THE QUEST OF RELIGION

THE QUEST OF RELIGION

BY

CHARLES E. RAVEN, D.D.

CANON OF LIVERPOOL AND
CHAPLAIN TO THE KING

LONDON
STUDENT CHRISTIAN MOVEMENT
32 RUSSELL SQUARE, W.C. I
1928

First published . . March 1928
Second Edition . . . May 1928

PRINTED IN GREAT BRITAIN BY
THE EDINBURGH PRESS, 9 AND 11 YOUNG STREET, EDINBURGH

TO

MY FRIEND AND FELLOW-WORKER

FREDERICK WILLIAM DWELLY

WITH LOVE AND JOY

To the Rev. Hugh Martin.

MY DEAR HUGH,

It is ten years since my first book, *What think ye of Christ?* was published, and five since you suggested that it might be revised and reprinted. Perhaps I have learned something since then; at least the times have changed; what was then written tentatively has now stood the test of a very varied experience and can be set out with a clearer conviction and a wider scope. At any rate a revision was impossible, and the present script must serve as a substitute.

Of course the book is a poor thing—chiefly because its theme is too high for me; partly too because in trying to be brief I have only succeeded in being scrappy. On two points of importance, the analogy between Jesus and the natural order, and the psychology of prayer and the group-mind, I have written at greater length in *The Creator Spirit*. On the doctrine of the Trinity the authorities for my interpretation are surveyed both there and in my *Apollinarianism*. But however inadequate the present treatment, you will agree that the subject is of supreme and unique importance. And I hope that although we differ widely in our denominational attachments there is almost nothing here with which you will disagree.

This is indeed the splendour of our time that the old barriers have ceased to separate us. Our faith, "whate'er our name or sign," is essentially one and the same : we can proclaim it without apology or equivocation or any sense of discord, contributing all that we have learned in our several churches and fellowships and movements to the enrichment of the one great Church which is the embodiment of the Spirit of Christ. For us in the Student Movement, and for a multitude of others, Anglicans or Free Churchmen or people without any denominational allegiance, the old things have passed away, and the reunion which some regard as a remote possibility is already a fact.

This is largely due to the new outlook which the scientific movement has produced. We have learned once more what the mystics of all ages have perceived —that reality is indeed infinite and in its essence indefinable, and that our creeds and doctrines, our art and philosophy, are at best approximations and hypotheses. The old insistence upon infallibilities involved a belief that the hypothesis was exactly identical with the reality, and is for us wholly impossible. The representatives of an earlier generation regard us as either sceptics or at least as grievously agnostic and unsettling. But in fact we are so used to testing and acting upon hypotheses that we accept the process for what it is, the natural and necessary condition of all knowledge. We may have only a half loaf, but it is more than sufficient to satisfy and sustain our souls; at least we have no intention of casting away what we have because we cannot here on earth get the whole.

Moreover, in view of the grandeur of God as we apprehend it in Christ and in the Universe we have little patience with the presumption which thinks that its little rules and formulæ are of ultimate and irreformable worth; and we are prepared to welcome rather than to exclude all those who are groping after religion. Certainly for you and me our differences are relatively so trivial that we could not dream of unchurching one another or challenging the validity of our " orders " or rejecting one another from the Supper of the Lord. And there are occasions when the refusal of our denominations to permit free interchange of pulpits and free admission to Communion seems so to divorce the outward from the inward as to taint all institutional religion with unreality if not with insincerity. Surely the time is near when we shall be allowed to confess our common membership and ministry in the Church and to share unreservedly in each and every act of Christian worship. Until then the "churches" will never recover their true character as the expression and instrument of spiritual fellowship.

Meanwhile for the work which you are doing to bring that day nearer and for your comradeship and kindness, my warmest gratitude.

Yours ever,

CHARLES E. RAVEN.

LIVERPOOL,
   Christmas, 1927.

CONTENTS

(*A*) THE KNOWLEDGE OF GOD

(*B*) GOD IN JESUS

(*C*) JESUS : GOD AND MAN

(*D*) MAN IN JESUS

THE QUEST OF RELIGION

(E) ETERNAL LIFE

THE QUEST OF RELIGION

(*A*) THE KNOWLEDGE OF GOD

I

THE EXPERIENCE OF THE ETERNAL

An ingenious American psychologist, influenced, no doubt, by the method of research by questionnaire, has recently compiled a list of forty-eight definitions of religion. As a means of arriving at a conclusion his labour was fruitless: he had to add two more of his own, and even these are not very satisfactory. But as a proof of the universal human need for religion, and of the various modes in which that need presents itself, his catalogue is full of interest. The definitions agree that religion is of supreme importance: they differ enormously in almost every other particular, ranging from simple and intriguing aphorisms like Professor Whitehead's "religion is what a man does with his *loneliness*," to elaborate statements of doctrine or of metaphysics. It is perhaps not surprising that whereas a century ago men described religion in terms of revelation and of a gift from God, nowadays they treat it from the standpoint of human experience.

All of us have a religion of some sort; for in the broadest sense religion is that by which a man lives, and in the process of growing up we all of us have to " come to terms with the universe," " range ourselves," find our place, however unconsciously, in the scheme of things. And in doing so we make our own certain impressions as to the purpose of life, certain standards for conduct, certain preferences and dominant desires which correspond, however vaguely, to a philosophy. Tucked away inside every human being is a more or less coherent ideal, developed out of his dreams and aspirations, his efforts and failures, coloured by his circumstances, but created not by them but by his own need to act in and upon them. It is his means of escape from isolation, his testimony to his membership in society, his recognition of and response to an existence larger than himself.

To trace out the various elements that enter into anyone's religion would be to construct a complete analysis of him. It may be gravely doubted whether any human life, however simple, can be thus fitted into a " museum of souls " or represented by a bare diagram. The whole is always greater than its parts, and there is something about it, a certain poise and completeness, emerging from its unity and undiscoverable by analytical methods. In any case, our concern is not with the varying constituents of any particular person's religion, but with certain experiences which enter into all religion and may not unreasonably be reckoned its essential quality. For there is one such factor which is being increasingly recognised by students, both of primitive and of modern man, by scientists and philosophers, as fundamental ; and it is a factor of which every one of us is more or less conscious.

It might be sufficient to quote the evidence of experts to prove that the basic element in religion is the sense of a reality that is outside ourselves and is not relative but absolute, of values which carry a compelling assent, of something fixed and eternal, abiding while all else may change, and giving to the transient its worth. Whether we call this experience mysticism, like the late Professor Gwatkin, or worship, like Professor Hocking, or the numinous, like Dr. Otto, or the emergence of deity, like Professor Alexander, we shall, I believe, mean the same thing ; and despite its title it is common to us all.

Put any ordinary person face to face with dawn in the mountains, and he will feel that here, behind the mere form and colour of the scene, is a beauty indescribable, complete, external to himself, the expression of a quality inherent in the very nature of things, a quality to which he must aspire. Or if he should be the kind of person who does not care for mountains, find for him whatever compels his admiration. Always beyond the thing itself there will be this sense of a larger and permanent beauty, a quality of perfection transcending but in some degree expressed by the particular object and giving to it its value.

Or test it on another plane. Anyone who thinks about life will soon come up against problems of whose solution he cannot be certain. He may persuade himself sophistically that there is no solution or even that there is no problem; but he will be haunted by a sense that the answer exists, and at times by the conviction that he apprehends it. Most of us must know moments when this glimpse of the truth of things becomes vivid.

Or if, being Englishmen, we are apt to dismiss the appeal of beauty as fanciful, or of truth as "high-brow," we can appeal to the more practical business of conduct. Here there is very general acknowledgment of a "categorical imperative," a compulsion which makes certain actions impossible, a command which is laid upon us and which we cannot but obey. This sense of a standard and an obligation to conform, of an "honour among thieves," of conscience, overlaid as it is by all sorts of conventions, shaped by upbringing, and distorted by twists in our own growth, yet appears ultimately as something outside ourselves, something independent of us. "Right is right," and after all the questionings there's the end of it: we can only resist its demands by outraging sanctions which lie very deep.

In such cases it is not easy to separate what may be called the eternal or ultimate element from more superficial factors due to habit, education and social pressure. Much of our æsthetic, intellectual and moral life is conditioned by standards borrowed from others, whether from the deliberate influence of teachers or from the acceptance of fashion: we take our judgments at second-hand. But it is a false philosophy which claims that we are wholly the creatures of our environment: in all of us there are certain direct appreciations which imply a sense of value innate and immediate. To take a simple instance: I am not an expert in architecture, and know nothing of the laws of proportion; but if I go into a schoolmaster's study and see there side by side photographs of the Parthenon and (say) of the similar temples at Paestum, I am at once aware that the former stirs me with a sense of its perfection, as a final and complete embodiment of beauty, whereas the other leaves me cold: I cannot in the latter case sense the eternal quality beneath the flaws (as it seems to me) of the technique. So too a Bach Mass, a few passages in the Iliad, the nineteenth psalm, certain flowers, the song of a willow-wren, the flight of a shearwater, these things have for me this same power to call out reverence: before them I can only "consider and bow the head."

For behind this talk of values lies an experience common to all normal folk, the experience commonly called mystic, the apprehension of "something beyond," something other than ourselves, before which we are humbled and awestruck, and yet with which we feel a kinship and a communion. Poets of all ages have described this sense, anthropologists have traced it back to the dawn of mankind, all simple people possess it, no lover has ever been without it : it is, as I believe, the source of our appreciation of value, the basis of the belief in immortality, the distinctive achievement of humanity. Without dogmatising about the lower animals, I should identify it with that breath which in the old story God breathed into man's nostrils when he became a living soul. It is the essential element in religion.

And despite the insistence of certain mystics on the loneliness of this communion of " the alone with the alone," it seems to me that its highest manifestations are attained in fellowship. It is a true principle of evolution that we have to become individuals before we can transcend our individuality, that we must have a self before we can lose and find it. And it is characteristic of adolescence that its religion should be solitary. Later on friendliness and comradeship become natural, and open up to us fuller opportunities of worship. The communion of the full-grown involves not only one's self and the Eternal, but the society of fellow-seekers. Religion demands God, but also for its development requires a church.

Yet the experience we have been describing lies behind any intellectual definition, behind dogma or philosophy. It is a conviction, an awareness, which affects our whole being. We can interpret it in terms of art and of knowledge and of conduct : but in doing so we must translate it, reducing its simplicity to levels of apprehension on which we can more easily analyse and describe it. It is the primary element : its presentation in terms of music and ritual, of creed and system, of morality and sociology, is secondary. And it is over these secondary matters that we enter the field of religious controversy.

II

ITS EXPRESSION FOR MANKIND

So far we have been concerned with a simple and universal experience, that man discovers in the universe a beauty, a reasonableness, a moral worth which he did not himself create, and which he accepts as inherent in the nature of things, and, further, that at his supreme moments he is aware of a definite relationship and union with the abiding reality that exists beyond the ebb and flow of phenomena. To express this experience in appropriate symbol, to give it intellectual explanation, to " live up " to it in his daily conduct, has always been a necessity for him. He cannot keep to himself what he has felt and known : yet he can only convey it in forms that approximate to the fact : he must needs translate it, by the best technique he can, into a shape wherein the infinite becomes tangible, intelligible, a guide to right conduct. The history of religions is the record of man's attempts to express religion in its appropriate art and philosophy and moral code.

From the dawn of human kind we can trace the beginnings of this effort. Crude drawings and idols, dancing and music, represent the primitive artist's conception of that which is the source of his raptures and terrors, of the nameless fascination and nameless awe with which nature affects him. Crude myths and quaint folk-lore are his early essays in speculative doctrine, as he feels the need to give an account of the origin and character of life. Crude taboos and a strange mixture of moral and ritual rules prove how he has tried to bring his ways into harmony with the mystery of which he is conscious. Anthropologists have classified for us a vast variety of such early religions, and are still arguing as to whether their resemblances are due to borrowing or to parallel development. Yet grotesque as they are, any simple and imaginative person who lives close to nature and has in him a spark of mysticism will understand how inevitably many of them suggest themselves. Idols, myths, codes of rules are native to us; however sophisticated we are, we cannot escape them. All we can do is to see that they represent as faithfully as possible the experience which constrains us to create them. Every religion has, and must have, its æsthetic, its doctrinal and its moral expressions. These will always be recognised by the more religious as secondary and in their measure inadequate; but no one can wholly dispense with them if he would explain to others the experience by which he is dominated. And if his whole life is influenced by religion, then, even if his art, his doctrine, his ethics be inadequate, he will by that which they express infect his fellows and achieve a real sharing of his experience with them.

And in thus interpreting the mystery mankind has seized upon its characteristic feature : it suggests the contact of life with life, of person with person, of man with God. The mystic experience, whatever our ultimate explanation of it may be, is most naturally described in terms of personality, of a supreme artist, or teacher, or law-giver, a Creator, a Saviour, an Inspirer. And this is due not only to the fact that personality represents the highest category of our experience, and therefore supplies most readily analogies for the interpretation of the mystery, but to the fact that mysticism has about it the quality of vital contact with One who cannot be fairly classified as impersonal. These two facts are worth further consideration.

(1) The experience in its fullness has, as we have urged, its æsthetic, intellectual and moral aspects : yet none of these is sufficient to embody it. To translate our consciousness of the eternal, no one faculty is competent ; only the whole personality, the unity to which emotion, reason and will belong, can be the medium. It is our whole self that is involved in our moments of worship ; it is as worship permeates and is expressed by the whole self that it becomes an abiding possession. To live eternally, to live in God — here is the goal of human development alike to Aristotle and to St. Paul. So long as we are men, no department of our man-hood will translate for us our apprehension of reality : only our complete and fully integrated humanity will

mirror for us deity. That is the basis of the Christian faith in the Incarnation and in the Church as the Body of Christ. It is a doctrine to which a study of worship inevitably leads. Perfect Man, if there is such perfection, would alone for us men be an adequate presentation of God.

(2) But are we justified in reaching the primary conclusion that the reality of which we are conscious is personal ? It has been argued that the testimony of the mystics is divided, and in particular that the Orientals generally refuse to describe reality in the language of theism. This is not the place in which to attempt a survey of the whole problem or a re-statement of the familiar and too readily rejected arguments for the existence of a personal God. But it may be urged that it is the Eastern concept of personality (which they identify with individuality, with limitation, and a space-time existence) that constrains them to disavow the personality of the divine. Many of us share their dislike of treating God as a glorified individual, or ascribing to Him the limitations of our own state. But we do not consider that such limitations constitute personality —rather indeed that true personality is not achieved until they are transcended. We would prefer to describe God as in this sense personal rather than super-personal or multi-personal ; but we should refuse absolutely to define Him as less than personal. And we believe that Christians in speaking of the Manhood of Jesus as universal and representative

(or sometimes but surely erroneously as impersonal) are contending for the conviction that in Him individuality was manifested at its highest power as personality.[1]

We can test this conception that the essence of religion is the experience of mysticism or worship, and that this experience, itself infinite, can only be given adequate expression when translated into terms of personality, since no lower category will do justice to it, by considering the quality of the experience itself. True mysticism as contrasted with the many spurious forms of rapture induced by drugs, by hypnosis, by auto-suggestion, or by herd-influence, produces in the mystic an intensifying of his whole vitality. His sensitiveness is heightened, his appreciation of beauty enriched, his intelligence quickened, his energy enlarged, his sense of fellow-ship deepened and expanded. He *lives* with a power based upon an inward peace, with a joy due to a conscious kinship with his fellows and with God. He is filled with the Spirit whose fruit is love, joy, peace, fortitude.

Yet with us, stunted and stained as we are, such fullness of life can only reach towards perfection as we share it with others. Those who are set free from loneliness by friendship, those who lose them-

[1] It is well to explain that individuality is applied to the self-conscious, self-centred unit, and that the individual attains personality as he develops relationships with others, replaces his selfishness by devotion to his fellows, and enters into the larger and richer life of the community.

selves in devotion to the society of their fellow-seekers after God, gain an insight into the meaning of life as worship which alone they cannot attain. Here as elsewhere the individual aspiration is only a first stage; beyond it lies the achievement of union in the blessed community with those who are united by a common experience of God. Ultimately only humanity itself can be the incarnation of the divine, the Christ that is to be, the fullness of that of which Jesus is the first-fruits. And it is in devotion to Him as the one adequate symbol and sacrament of God that we can rise to the fulfilment of our true end, life in God: by love of Him we become like Him, one with Him, in Whom is God reconciling the world to Himself. That is the Christian faith.

But is Jesus then the true translation into human terms of the mystery?

III

THE TESTS OF THAT EXPRESSION

HITHERTO we have urged that there is as the core of religion and the supreme achievement of man an experience of contact with reality; that behind and beyond and yet within phenomena is something, someone, that cannot be described in terms of less and more, that is, ultimate, eternal, divine. This experience mankind strives to translate into a symbolism appropriate to it. Such symbolism can be found in the three departments of man's activity: art, thought and action, the æsthetic, the intellectual and the moral spheres, can all be used to embody it. Fully expressed, it must satisfy our highest aspirations in all these directions. Yet the experience is too deep for any sectional interpretation. Only life, only a personality permeated by it, can translate it adequately for us. The Christian claims that in Jesus Christ we have the sole adequate incarnation of reality, of God.

If this claim is to be maintained there are certain conditions that the claimant must fulfil, and these can best be stated in three headings. No interpretation of the real character of the universe that fails to satisfy these three will be satisfactory.

(1) It must stand the test of value; we must find in it beauty, and truth, and goodness. Human nature demands it, and bases its demand upon the very nature of things. Any impartial study of the universe will disclose as its most obvious quality beauty. I was lately looking over a large series of moths that I collected years ago, and was almost overwhelmed by the subtlety, variety and harmony of their colouring. Alike in detail and as a whole, each one is perfect, a work of art consummate and complete. And everywhere, both in structure and in movement, the impression is the same. Awe and wonder, joy and pity, laughter and tears, here is that which stirs and transcends them all: in common things that we take for granted, in flowers and birds, woodland and sea, earthquake and sunrise, is food for every need of our emotional life.

And the impression of beauty leads on to an impression of meaning. Here is no purposeless lavishing of art: behind form lies function. We see and are curious, and our minds get to work. The little glimpses that we can get of the meaning of it all, convince us that there is reason in the universe; we cannot but be fascinated by the riddles that are yet unanswered, by the master-riddle, which is God. Whatever the ultimate explanation, the universe is so constructed that reasoning power and the quest for truth have been developed within it: it is rational, orderly, a school for the discipline of its children's minds.

And deeper still there is the conviction of goodness. The universe has enabled the evolution of a moral sense; and we, its youngest children, have in us, however overlaid, a passion for righteousness. It is not only God who has looked out upon creation and found it all very good. We may wrestle with its problems, and be aghast at its horrors and be tortured by its ruthlessness, but "though He slay me, yet will I trust Him" is man's authentic confession. On the whole, and trying honestly to face the woe of the world, we should reject any interpretation of it which did not satisfy our appreciation of the good. If we cannot fully understand, at least we accept the universe.

(2) This last paragraph has raised the substance of our second condition. Any adequate translation of reality must throw light on the fundamental problem: it must help us to understand suffering. The evidence of the part played by struggle in the creative process has reinforced for us our own experience of pain, and for very many has cast doubts upon the whole character of God. Recent research, both in challenging the denial of the inheritance of acquired characteristics and in drawing attention to the importance of social qualities, of tenderness and loyalty and co-operative effort, in the story of evolution, has set us free from the pessimism of the great Victorians. But if we no longer see "nature red in tooth and claw," no generation has been more violently convinced of the horror and cruelty and lust which accompanies the march of life. "Why

all this pain?" is a cry from the heart: and no religion which has not its explanation to offer will appeal to any save the superficial or the childish. For the problem of suffering, more I believe than the somewhat kindred problem of evil, distresses the hearts and bewilders the minds of us all.

(3) Nature appeals to every one of her human children: each in our own way we come to terms with the universe: each finds in its manifold variety some aspect of special significance, some particular element which is his avenue into the central mystery. Personal, national and racial temperaments differ enormously: sex, surroundings, social environment create broad types of culture and outlook: yet we are all at home in the world. Any translation of reality must have the characteristic mark of universality upon it. It must not be confined in its influence by geographical or temporary peculiarities. Beauty, truth, goodness, these are timeless, even if man's efforts to attain them are marred by local and ephemeral traits; they testify to something that transcends our fashions and our philosophies. If personality, if a perfect man, is for us the mirror of God, that personality must itself surpass the limits of the individual: in it there must be "neither Greek nor Jew, neither male nor female."

These three conditions amount to this, that if we can find any presentation of the eternal of which we can say, "This is for me God," such presentation must exhibit the same qualities which we discover in our highest appreciation of the universe. Nature not only confronts us with problems, it suggests certain hints of a solution. If Jesus is what we mean when we call Him Son of God, we shall expect to find Him raising these same questions and giving us a far clearer and more intelligible answer to them. The universe is too vast for us to disclose and apprehend its message; in the microcosm of a human life we should be able to see the whole vast field reduced to a scale in which we can study it. When the early believers called Jesus " God's mystery," they meant that here was the representative and symbolic event into which was condensed and from which was illuminated the whole range of God's nature and activities. Just as at Eleusis the mystic drama was believed to express to the initiate the true nature of existence, so in Jesus men claimed that here was the eternal manifested in a human life, a life that satisfied man's craving for beauty and truth and goodness, that explained for him the facts of suffering and of sin, and that appealed irresistibly to all who were of human kind, Jesus the same yesterday and to-day and for ever, the image of the unseen, the way, the truth and the life.

And if it is urged that this statement leaves out what is ordinarily meant by salvation, redemption, or forgiveness, I would reply that forgiveness means only union with God, that redemption is liberty to realise our own true end, which is life in Him, that salvation is not the escape from hell but the attainment here and now of heaven; that Jesus relied, not upon prohibitions but upon aspirations, upon love not fear; and that any true presentation of religion must put God and not our own sins first.

(*B*) GOD IN JESUS

IV

JESUS AND THE ETERNAL VALUES

THAT religion, or man's experience of the eternal, can be expressed for us men in terms of human life more adequately than by any other medium would probably not be disputed. Art, philosophy, ethics, these are only partial expressions of personal experience; they are elements discoverable by analysis of that which includes and transcends them; and the whole is greater than its parts.

The more disputable part of the Christian claim is that which identifies the perfect Man with Jesus, and maintains not merely that He excels other men in the degree of His achievement, but so embodies the supreme values as to be in fact God incarnate. It is not enough to point to the evidence of the impact of His personality upon contemporaries whose whole tradition made the idea of an incarnation an unthinkable blasphemy, though it is at least significant that, while receiving from the rulers of His nation the martyrdom which Plato had foretold for the perfectly righteous, He was acclaimed by those who knew Him as Son of God. Nor can we decide the issue by pointing to His creative influence through the centuries, an influence whose magnitude it is almost impossible to overestimate. We must test the claim for ourselves in the light of the best scholarship and our own highest experience. Have we in Jesus such beauty, such truth, such goodness as satisfies our powers of appreciation, and constrains us to the sense of worship which is our homage to achieved perfection?

There are two warnings that must be borne in mind, the first affecting ourselves as critics, the second concerning the portrait of Jesus that has come down to us. We cannot indeed escape the responsibility of a verdict : but who are we that we should judge? Every one of us is imperfect, and most of us are unconscious of our more serious imperfections. Modern education and the increasing complexity of life so fosters specialisation and lop-sided growth that " the full-grown man " is hard to find. It is almost inevitable that whole spheres of experience lie outside my knowledge, that certain elements in life which may be claimed as essential to perfection are beyond my range and arouse in me distrust and even repulsion. Many of us twenty years ago were irritated by the gentleness which our elders emphasised in Jesus : we either rejected Him, or on enquiring found in Him a heroic virility to which they had been blind. To-day the younger genera-tion is obviously reacting against the concept of Jesus as the revolutionary adventurer : their seniors have emphasised His violence so strongly as to

c

obscure His sensitiveness and sympathy. Each of us then, in proportion as we are ourselves undeveloped, will find in Him elements for which we have small power of appreciation ; and when we do so must ask ourselves whether the fault is in Him or in ourselves. Is it because I am myself a bit of an ecclesiastic that I find His denunciation of the Pharisees hard to reconcile with His refusals to denounce ? Was it my own prejudice in favour of slow and ordered evolution that made me stumble at His use of Apocalyptic until I was plunged into the war and discovered that certain experiences can only be described in terms of darkened sun and falling heavens ?

The second warning has to do with the character of the records of Jesus. Then as now the limitations of us others have to be reckoned with. If I cannot see more than a part of Him, the evangelists themselves can only tell what their knowledge enabled them to apprehend, and must tell it through the medium of their own outlook. It is the task of scholarship, here as in all historical research, to estimate the extent and character of the personal equation of an author, and to discriminate in his work between the objective and subjective elements. It was natural that, in reaction against the traditional view which held every Gospel and every text to be equally authentic, critics should at first have laid such stress upon discrepancies as to suggest a doubt as to whether we could ever know Jesus as He was. We are still too prone to speak as if the Jesus of

St. Mark, and of Q., and of St. Luke, and of the Fourth Gospel were independent and antagonistic. But the process so admirably described by Dr. Schweitzer, which seeks truth by way of a series of alternatives, has obviously resulted in something like a *reductio ad absurdum*, and critical study having now learnt how to appraise the several documents is returning towards more synthetic methods. Already we refuse to regard St. Mark and Q. as irreconcilable : we are discovering that the apocalyptic is complementary to the ethical : we shall soon be willing and able to use the Johannine interpretation, and, I believe, to recognise that it contains matter of primary historical worth. But the student who would deal fairly with the claim of Jesus cannot neglect an enquiry into the sources and character of our knowledge. He will find good reason to believe that certain episodes, for example the raising of Jairus' daughter, the destruction of the Gadarene swine, the walking on the water, and others, do not bear the significance traditionally ascribed to them, and that others, notably the birth narratives in the First Gospel, the promise to St. Peter, and many of the eschatological sayings, are of very doubtful authenticity. It is not that criticism can be used as an easy means of excising or explaining away what we do not understand, but that there are in fact elements of very varying reliability in the records, and that before we decide about Jesus it is our duty to see Him as clearly and truthfully as we can. There remains vastly more material for a portrait than scholars of a generation ago were ready to admit.

How far then does Jesus satisfy the test of value?

Beauty.—Can any impartial person who has any *flair* for greatness in art read the Sermon on the Mount, or the parable of the Prodigal Son, or any other of the poems of Jesus, without feeling that peculiar thrill of awe and rapture which is our response to supreme beauty? And for us His art has been staled by familiarity, obscured by homiletics, caricatured by doctrinal interpretation. We can hardly recover any freedom of appreciation, or let the original creation have its way with us. Yet even so, behind the narcotic effect of " devotional " reading, and the distraction of controversy, His beauty stands out for us as it has done for the artists of all time. Nor is it simply a beauty of utterance. His words may be poetry; His life is the supreme poem. He lives beauty. Simplicity, naturalness, poise, harmony, grace, variety, range-test Him by what canon you will, and He satisfies it. Here is art like nature's own, art by which joy and suffering, terror and mirth alike are evoked and transcended, art in which the *mysterium tremendum et fascinans* has its supreme interpretation.

Truth.—Here is more difficult ground: for we are apt to degrade truth till it means little more than accuracy of statement, and so to criticise Jesus because He did not teach us knowledge of medicine or sanitation, of evolution, or literary criticism, or aeronautics. Truth is not knowledge : it is order, reason, rationality, the interpretation of reality in terms of accurate symbolism, the comprehension of the eternal in a coherent, intellectual presentation. It is irrelevant to our enquiry that Jesus accepted the Davidic authorship of the Psalter, or even contemporary ideas of demonology, just as it is that He lived in Palestine or spoke Aramaic. Did He enable men to form true views of life ? Did He set them thinking along right lines ? Did He give a faithful account of that existence which, as Socrates would say, is a matter not of opinion but of rational intelligence ? Test the answer where you will ; test it, for example, in the Beatitudes, or the ethical teaching, or the paradoxes of life lost and gained, or the answers to His critics, or His doctrine of God. Is not this true ? Does it not give us the conviction that here is indeed the key to knowledge, the solution of riddles, the exposition of a reality which in Him we can begin to understand ? For many of us at least His utterances, and still more His life, have a ring of finality about them : we feel as we do when for a moment nature seems to reveal to us her secret : we apprehend that this is real, even if we cannot set it down in a series of propositions. Not for nothing did His followers call Him " teacher," and claim that His

37

Spirit would lead them into all truth. What we can learn of Him convinces us that they were right.

Goodness.—It is probably the moral grandeur of Jesus that most compels worship ; His embodiment of love that draws men to Him. There are some who have fixed upon one aspect alone, and have accused Him either of " slave morality," or of " excessive violence," of being too humble or too arrogant. It is indeed striking how when one interpreter arises and gives us his verdict, another almost immediately draws attention to an exactly opposite character. We have seen Jesus depicted as feminine and masculine, lonely and sociable, tolerant and minatory, quietist and rebel. Of no other character, save God, has mankind given such a variety of accounts. It might appear that the original was a mass of contradictions. Study Him and see. Out of the many facets of His personality is built up a unity congruous with the highest that we know, consistent so far as we can measure consistency, overwhelming in the scale and scope of its quality ; Man in a universal sense that no other has approached, the fulfilment of every worthy element in our race. I have confessed that there are aspects of Him which are difficult : for me at least certain of His deeds and words were for years definite stumbling-blocks, and I had to face my doubts as honestly and weigh the evidence as fully as I could. At least I am sure that the enquiry was as unbiased as I could make it, that it started with a definite desire to overthrow the orthodox conclusion, and that it led to satisfaction, to confession, to adoration. For me, here as elsewhere, He has the value of God, is the Incarnate of God, the personality in whom Beauty, Truth and Goodness are supremely and uniquely revealed.

And for us God embodied in Man becomes an object not only of worship but of love. There may be mystics whose consciousness of the eternal has quickened for a moment into an adoration for which love is not too strong a word ; but the history of religion makes it plain that such souls are rare. Too often such a relationship is mere emotion-alism—a swooning into the arms of the infinite characterised by little that is in any real sense excellent. Judged by its effects it fails to produce any enhancement of vitality or to arouse an activity of service, but remains a sterile passivity. God in Christ is not merely the satisfaction of desire, the object of a blessed but fruitless contemplation : He is creative, energising, regenerating : He not only unifies and sublimates, He inspires and con-strains to the fulfilment of His will. If it is true that the work of God is that we believe on Him Whom He hath sent, it is also true that such belief involves a surrender to the ever-active, ever-redemptive Spirit ; it is a dedication not to contemplation but to the Cross, a love which com-pels us to go and do likewise, to share and to fulfil

God's eternal task of winning the world unto
Himself. Jesus is not only the expression of deity:
He is the instrument by which deity becomes
operative in us.

V

JESUS AND THE PROBLEM OF SUFFERING

ONE supreme problem has always confronted mankind since first he began to ask questions about the meaning and nature of the world in which he lived. " Why all this pain ? " is a cry that every human being must utter, a question so insistent as to demand from the least inquisitive some sort of reply. Propitiatory rites, demon-worship, dualism complete or veiled, doctrines of a Fall, of an angry God, of a ruthless necessity—in a multitude of forms we have tried to console and fortify one another, and to justify the ways of an inscrutable Providence. And to-day, when the element of struggle and suffering in the evolutionary process has been so powerfully emphasised, and when thirteen years of agony have left our hearts wrung and our nerves strained, it is to many almost a mockery to talk of a God of love, a God like Jesus, as the source and reality of existence. Unless Jesus can help us here, He cannot receive or sustain our homage.

It is a theme on which only those who have themselves suffered dare speak, and where none may speak glibly. The easy optimism of conventional piety is futile : so is the well-meant cheerfulness of those lucky but useless folks who have no sense of tragedy. The facile consolation, spoken or written, " the empty chaff well-meant for grain," that appears in hymns and sermons, has probably alienated more souls from the churches than any other single cause. He who would help his fellows here must bear in his own body the print of nails and spear. It is because He can say " Is any sorrow like unto My sorrow ? " it is because He can ask " Can ye drink of the cup that I drink of ? " that men have found in Jesus a Saviour. It is by right of the Cross that He reigns.

To say so is to claim that He not only illuminates the meaning of suffering but that He vindicates its place in the scheme of things, and demands of us a change of outlook so complete as to overthrow all our standards of success, of pleasure, of ambition. Can this claim be made good ?

(1) The first lesson of the Cross is that the suffering of the innocent is the result of the inherited insensitiveness, the blind prejudices, the self-complacency and conservatism, not less than of the deliberate cruelty and greed, of mankind. Pharisees, Sadducees, Herod, Pilate had all excellent reasons for doing what they did : they being what they were, the whole drama moved inevitably to its tremendous climax ; men crucified their own true Manhood because they could not free themselves from the obsession of ambitions and fears,

of habit and inheritance. The tragedy of it has the universality of supreme art. Here, focused to a point in Calvary, is the pain of the world. The Christian facing a row of beds in a hospital or a queue of dockers at a Labour Exchange, finds himself murmuring, " They are punished for our transgressions," and " The Lord has laid on them the iniquity of us all." He sees in tortured bodies and starved souls, the marks of the Lord Jesus : and remorse for his own share in their crucifixion cuts him to the heart. And if human woe is thus seen anew as the outcome of man's ignorance and sloth and acquiescence in inherited wrong, the same light shines back upon the suffering of the animal world. Life differs from the inanimate in its power of self-determination : the amœba, unlike the blob of colloid, has a capacity for alternate response. Our freedom is bought at the price of mistakes, and mistakes involve always and everywhere more or less of calamity for the race : the innocent pay in blood.

(2) So far we see only the remorseless rule of necessity—a judgment just indeed but grim ; and the sense of an appalling imprisonment crushes in us the seeds of pride. But the Cross, if it plunges us into despair, does not leave us there ; with penitence and consciousness of our impotence, comes encouragement and triumphant release. For out of evil springs good ; through suffering there is revealed love and love victorious. The

vindication of Calvary is that in fact it sets men like Simon Peter, or me, free. No sooner do we realise our bondage than the fetters are loosed from our limbs. Jesus by His death so manifested the power of love, so called out sympathy, devotion and passionate loyalty, that the men whose adventure had seemed to end in disillusionment were reborn with a vitality incredibly larger and a fellowship immeasurably deeper than they could else have achieved.

Those who crucified the Son of Man found Him far more creative in His death than He had been in His life. The Gospel, which had hitherto aroused hope and interest, now displayed an energy which accomplished the transformation of human nature. Pilate may have forgotten his victim : the world has not done so : indeed it remembers the Procurator only from his connection with Jesus.

The truth is that, as with St. Joan, so far more mightily with Jesus, martyrdom was not the end but the beginning. The testimony sealed in blood prevailed. Men's consciences were aroused, their sympathies quickened, their aspirations revived. Mankind rose again from its old self to newness of life. The prejudices blindly accepted could now be challenged, the fears tyrannising over the soul were seen to be groundless : complacency had led to catastrophe, complacency was shattered : mankind shook itself from stagnation and set out on the march. And Jesus, whatever we may think of the post-resurrection appearances, was obviously not dead but living, active, present, the greatest creative and regenerative influence in history.

So with mankind—were it not for pain we should have been mere Robots, without sensibility, without friendship, sterile and joyless. It is the recognition of pain, the effort to escape and allay it, that calls out altruism : pity is the twin-sister of joy, and they are the inspiration of all unselfish service. And as we trace back the evolution of life, we find that an increase of sensibility is always the meaning of development, that struggle and suffering are creative, that by the discipline of trial and error, trial and triumph, along a road marked by the bones of an exceeding great army, the slow advance is won. Not indeed that there is pain until a relatively high level has been reached : the insects, the crustaceans, the amphibians, the reptiles, these seem hardly to feel pain at all ; in the birds, as anyone knows who has seen a winged pheasant run off at once regardless of the shock, pain in our sense of the word is insignificant ; even among mammals sensitiveness is relatively slight. But throughout it is the loss of life, the elimination of the unfit, that plays the largest part in progress ; and where pain begins there is a heightening of all the faculties, and what was before an unconscious effort to survive shows signs of planning, of adjustment of means to end, of conscious comradeship, of dawning sympathy. $\pi\alpha\theta\epsilon\hat{\iota}\nu$ $\mu\alpha\theta\epsilon\hat{\iota}\nu$, says the Greek aphorism : suffering is learning.

(3) And if so, if indeed God chasteneth every son whom He receiveth, then those may well be the failures in life who achieve what the world calls success. Comfort, prosperity, luxury—these are the perils of the soul. "How hardly shall they that have riches enter into God's Kingdom" becomes a tremendous truth. Riches are not evil in themselves : Jesus never said that they were : but those who possess them, just because they are sheltered from suffering, are liable to become insensitive, complacent, callous, dead. Any man of good sense would admit that the educative forces of the soul are to be found in the great happenings of life, that pain and the presence of death, along with love and parenthood, are the occasions of growth. And any man who knows the poor will find among them a comradeship, a generosity, a reality which puts him to shame. It is not that circumstances create character, or that suffering does not ever break and brutalise. But from a Christian standpoint it may be doubted whether the spiritual state of the slums is ever as near damnation as that of Mayfair. At least it is significant that Jesus condemned not the publican and the harlot but those who knew that they were righteous and despised others, and that in the days of its glory the Church contained not many wise nor noble nor mighty. It is those of us whose lives lie in smooth and pleasant places, sheltered from tragedy and oppression, who should ask ourselves how far we understand or are taking up the Cross.

"Is it nothing to you, all ye that pass by?" is only another way of saying, "Inasmuch as ye did it not": it is the sentence upon those who have made the great refusal.

And for the Church, it is not by her dignity and pomp, her glory of art and ceremonial, eloquence and enthusiasm that she will prove her claim: if she is indeed the Body of Christ, she will show the signs of the Passion, the crown of thorns and the pierced hands and feet. Our small quarrels about tradition and orthodoxy, precedent and pride of place, reveal how far we have fallen from the austere standards of our Lord. "He that is great among you, let him be the servant"; man's highest vocation is to give his life a ransom for many. The Church too must die, and die daily, that she may live.

VI

THE UNIVERSALITY OF JESUS

THERE are times in the religious life of most of us when the claim of Jesus seems an incredible presumption. In the vast, the inconceivably vast stretches of space and time which modern science reveals, among the infinite riches of living organisms, over the agelong vistas of human history, can we dare to fix a span of thirty years as the epoch when the eternal God was manifested in the flesh? Can the particular in any case reveal the universal? Can a Jew of the first century be uniquely Son of God? The whole idea seems a remnant of mythology, a survival from a primitive era when man could call himself the lord of creation, and find sufficient scope for worship in homely cults and childish creeds. Surely the belief in an Incarnation is too pitifully anthropocentric: surely the Crucified only holds our homage by the bonds of ancient habit: surely it is time that we put away the relics of a credulous adolescence. We shall do so reverently: the nursery and its toys have a peculiar sanctity: and it was good that in our youth we should have such pretty and poignant playthings. We shall spend a sigh upon the Galilean as the tribute to His share in our upbringing. But in the twentieth century we have grown out of such conceits: God, if any God there be, will be found on a scale commensurate with light-years and electrons, the units of measurement, great and small, which now serve as " the reed of a man."

So Celsus, the second-century critic of Christianity, whose acute mind raised most of the objections usually put forward as modern, after devoting the first part of his book to an attack upon Jesus, in the second dismissed the whole problem on the ground that, whatever Jesus was, the idea of God as having any special regard for man was mere bumptiousness on man's part. Even if Jesus was the ideal man, this did not involve His divinity: as well might the frogs announce that their noblest specimen was the Son of God. The claim of Jesus, whatever His character, is a ridiculous absurdity.

It is the sort of objection specially calculated to impress those who are bewildered by new discoveries or influenced by reaction against conventionality. It has an air of humility about it that is subtly flattering to the vanity of the man in the street: and it needs no intelligence and no knowledge to endorse it. " Of course I'm not a philosopher and don't profess to understand either the arguments of scientists or the sophistries of theologians. But I am at least humble enough to see how puerile is all this talk about an incarnation. Myth, my dear sir, myth and moonshine—well enough for women and children, but I'm a man and have put away childish things." That is a common attitude, and does not look nearly so silly as it really is.

It is silly just because it is based upon assumptions that are wholly illogical. The size and complexity, the nature and composition, the age and duration of the universe as revealed by the physical sciences have in fact no connection at all with the fundamentals of religion. Religion is concerned not with quantity but with quality, with man's apprehension of values and of a Being of whose " supreme reality he is convinced by the love which it awakens and the new life which it imparts." [1] If our fresh knowledge has immensely enlarged our understanding of the scope of the divine energy, if in relation to the world it has humbled us, we remain men, and as men are still, as in Aristotle's time, concerned with the business of " living eternally." The validity of my experience of God is not affected by my views on astronomy or on evolution, unless by them I am led into the error of the materialist and attempt to explain or explain away the whole in terms of certain of the parts into which I have analysed it.

Yet, if mechanistic interpretations of nature fail thus to explain reality, does not the Christian claim fail on exactly the same grounds? Can a

[1] Ward, *Essays*, p. 355.

part, Jesus, be an adequate interpretation of the whole? Can a Jew of the first century be in any true sense God? Even if it be admitted that man's knowledge of God is real, can a particular man express the full content of that knowledge? Is Jesus and the revelation in Him universal for humanity?

In reply the three following points may be urged: (1) that mankind has not advanced beyond, indeed has not begun to reach, the level of Jesus; (2) that men of the most various temperaments and races, indeed, "all nations and languages," have found satisfaction in Him; (3) that He appeals to men as nature does, at once fulfilling and transcending, inspiring and educating their highest aspirations.

(1) The past century has done a grand work in recovering for us a true understanding of the meaning and character of Jesus. In helping us to see Him as He was in the days of His flesh, it has shown up the extent to which His religion has been degraded by that which has been preached in His name. Quite obviously the Church, both in its doctrine and in its practice, has often fallen grievously away from His Spirit: it is easy to set out a series of contrasts between Jesus and the Christianity of the Church, contrasts as violent as those which Marcion noted between the God of the Old Testament and the God of the New. We may urge that the history of Christianity has

been an evolution, that the way of life that Jesus revealed had to be interpreted, analysed, systematised, by men of very varying capacities to meet the circumstances of special epochs. In doing so growth was sectional : the simplicity and harmony of the original was upset : mistakes were made in concession to worldly needs. No task is so urgent as to realise clearly and proclaim effectively the extent of our failure and the means of reformation. But that the comparison of the Church of to-day with the religion of Jesus denotes our failure, only proves how much He surpasses His followers. No genuine student of Church history will doubt that the bulk of the developments, even if they were degradations of His teaching, were sincerely meant by men whose desire was to act in accordance with His Spirit. Where they fell, it was through misunderstanding, not malice : He was too great for them, great as many of them were. If the contrast fills us with shame that we have so caricatured our Master, it fills us also with joy that He so vastly transcends His disciples. It is His grandeur rather than the errors of His Church that impresses the historian. "Christianity," said Martineau, "understood as the personal religion of Jesus Christ, stands clear of all perishable elements and realises the true relation between man and God." [1]

(2) If all normal men, despite the vast differences of cultural and racial outlook, have in common

[1] *The Seat of Authority in Religion*, p. 651.

and fundamentally an agreement as to the eternal values, and if Jesus is, as we have urged, the unique embodiment of those values, we should expect to find that His appeal, rightly understood, was universal. " Yea, heaven is everywhere at home " : Jesus, like God, will have everywhere His worshippers.

Universality of appeal is indeed a characteristic of His Gospel from the first. The Jewish apologist who wrote or edited the First Gospel, the Greek doctor who wrote the Third and the Acts, St. Peter, St. Paul, and the Fourth Evangelist had little in common save Jesus : but in Him they found satisfaction and fellowship. In the early Church similar evidence confronts us : Oriental mystics like Bardaisan, Platonists like Clement of Alexandria, legalists and puritans like Tertullian, slaves and statesmen, warriors and anchorites, Assyrians and Numidians, Goths and Romans, alike bowed the knee to the Nazarene and acclaimed Him Son of God : and if their appreciation of Him was partial and inadequate, at least it was sincere and the noblest element in their lives. The conviction that His Manhood represents the general perfection of human nature lies behind the significant refusal of the Church to call Him an individual man, and is the motive of the irritating doctrine of His impersonal humanity.

And here, too, recent studies have confirmed earlier testimony. The great variety of the " lives " of Jesus published during the past decade proves at least the power of His influence upon men of all types : the Tory " die-hard," the revolutionary Socialist, the man of letters, the man of business, adventurers and administrators, pedants and pietists, unite to pay homage to Him, and in doing so rise, however little, above the limitations of their outlook. We may feel that none of them does justice to Him, indeed that their portraits of Him are scarcely more than the projection of their own highest selves : but between them they create in us the impression of a figure which if many-sided is only so because it is too vast for any of us to grasp entire. Seeing it, we feel that those psychologists are right who claim that Jesus is alone normal and normative Man, that we others are defective beside Him, and that we can test and regulate our development by comparison with His full-orbed completeness.

Nor is the evidence true only of the white races. Missionaries in Asia and Africa endorse the witness of Europe. Other peoples, though they reject the creeds and organisation by which Jesus has been interpreted in the West, find that, if Christianity repels, Jesus attracts. On " the Indian road," as in China or Uganda or pagan England, those whose lives and words speak of Jesus discover the power of His appeal. Men who hate everything else that the West can give, when they have stripped Him of the trappings that Europe has laid on Him, find in Him the desire of all nations, the common ideal, the common Saviour of humanity.

(3) It is not for us to dogmatise about the finality for all time and every creature of the revelation in Jesus.

> " For God has other Words for other worlds,
>   But for this world the Word of God is Christ."

That is enough for us. Yet, believing that the supreme experiences of mankind have an absolute character, and that those experiences find their perfect manifestation in Jesus, we must feel that His perfection is not relative but eternal, that He is not merely God for us, but God in every sense in which we can understand deity. And indeed, as we come to study and appreciate Him more truly, we discover in Him the same combination of many-sidedness and congruity that we find in nature. In both cases it is easy to see special aspects, aspects which in isolation look inconsistent with the rest : in both cases, as we try to take a full view of the whole, we find that though it transcends our grasp, it yet impresses us with a sense of unity and har-mony. As I learn to see God, not only in the sunrise but in the earthquake, not only in the lilies and in the birds but in the toadstool and in the tiger, I begin to feel more by intuition than by reason that His activity is one and indivisible, His character a synthesis vast and yet consistent. So with Jesus, as the several hues of His person-ality are disclosed to me, the sense grows in me that I am in the presence of the very light of the world, of a light so brilliant that I can see only part

55

of its spectrum. He becomes for me what He was to Clement, " the many-coloured wisdom of God," or what He was to the author of Hebrews, " the effulgence of His glory." And my response must be to " walk in the light."

(C) JESUS: GOD AND MAN

VII

JESUS THE MYSTERY OF GOD

THAT Jesus is for us men the unique expression
of the eternal, does not in itself explain the nature
of His influence upon mankind. For He could be
this, and yet be no more than a memory belonging
to the first century. To many of His followers,
ancient or modern, He is doubtless just an historical
character : they look back to the Gospels as the
record of a theophany, and to Him as the example
of a perfect life once lived upon earth. Their faith in
Him may be real, their devotion intense : but it is
not quite the sort of faith or of devotion which
changed the life of Saul of Tarsus or sent the
Christian message flaming across the world.

If the experience of His closest followers is to
be trusted, Jesus is not a dead pattern, but a living
friend. He spoke to the Twelve in Galilee in the
days of His flesh : He spoke to Saul on the road to
Damascus and, according to tradition, to St. Peter
at the Latin Gate : and throughout Christian history
there is similar evidence of His presence. Indeed,
in St. Paul's case, the conviction that Jesus is

" risen from the dead " and still vividly active is
the reason why the Apostle cares so little to know
Him " after the flesh " or to refer back to the details
of His ministry. Jesus is with him in Ephesus or
Corinth, and present guidance is better than
memory or tradition. Jesus is with him and alive
for evermore, the same yesterday, to-day, and
always.

There can be no question that this intense
conviction of the nearness of Jesus was the secret
of the power of the Christian life in the early days.
Those men loved their Lord with a love utterly
selfless and therefore utterly satisfying; and loving
Him as God they knew that such love was eternal
life. Their devotion was not the sentimental and
erotic passion which makes a hysterical Jesus-
worship so weak and false; to them He was "God's
mystery," the key to the treasury of the unseen
world, the point at which the diffused gleams of
spiritual light were condensed and directed into
a steady ray. Their vision of the world was
illuminated by Him: by Him its problems were
solved and its true nature revealed. There are
moments in the experience of us all when for a
little space God is so real to us that conventional
standards and self-centred habits and all the compli-
cation of our disharmony are forgotten: we look
out upon the world with the candour of a child
and find it natural, simple, almost intelligible:
we seem to comprehend the whole of it, and
behold it is all very good. Those who have passed

into the presence of death and got beyond ambition and fear, thus walk the earth as if it were heaven : its events have the fascination of a great drama in which the *revenant* plays his part, but from which his real self stands aloof : he sees and controls his fate with a freedom due to his detachment, throwing himself into the joy of living with a thrill of wonder, and yet neither overwhelmed nor even absorbed by events. So the early Christian, initiated by Jesus into the heavenlies, lived with the gaiety and courage, the sympathy and liberty of a child of God sojourning for a span upon the earth. In Jesus all was made new : this world was an episode and death an irrelevance : reality was Christ, and circumstances were real only because He had given them meaning. God and Jesus were identified not dogmatically nor philosophically, but in the experience of the believer : for the fleeting apprehension of God which gives to Plotinus or to Wordsworth his sense of the harmony of nature was for them quickened by love into an abiding mysticism which they could express not in a treatise or a poem but in daily conduct by living eternally. Theologians may argue indefinitely as to the Pauline doctrine of the Trinity, or deplore the naïve heterodoxies of Hermas or of the Catacombs. Jesus, the Christ, the Spirit of Jesus, the Spirit of God, the Holy Spirit, God—these are not subtle discriminations, employed with systematic consistency, but random names used interchangeably to denote the supreme fact that Jesus was

God and God just Jesus everywhere, and that man's universal experience of vague cosmic emotion had for the Christian been intensified into a clear and permanent communion, a love given and returned. We may describe this experience as union with God, but with God conceived and apprehended in terms of Jesus; or as union with Jesus, with Jesus universalised and glorified, filling for the mystic the whole scale of the divine perfection. In either case God and Jesus as the objects of adoration are not separable, are not two but one. The concept of God as a colourless, passionless, remote abstraction and of Jesus as the mere Nazarene, as the gentle and beloved peasant-prophet, these have disappeared. There remains the characteristically Christian concept of God as Love, of God to whom man's attitude of worship is enriched by feelings of kinship, trust, devotion, God whose realm is still the universe but whose face is the face of Jesus. With such a God mankind is indeed a family and the earth a home.

A careful study of the religious experience of Christians to-day would probably reveal a similar identification as normal. It is easy and interesting to notice that two types can be distinguished. There are those whose highest moments of communion are associated with the Father: Jesus to them is the Way, by whom they have their access to the divine; but the cosmic rather than the incarnate aspect of God dominates their spiritual outlook. Others as definitely find Jesus the centre of their faith : in their rapture He is so vividly present, so plainly visualised, as to leave no room for anything beyond or behind Him. The difference would seem to be temperamental, the intellectual is usually in the former category, the emotional in the latter : the one may easily become somewhat cold and academic, the other is in danger of sentimentalising religion. Each element has its place in Christianity, and the fully integrated believer will combine and harmonise both types of experience. Indeed to many of us the distinction ceases to be evident. God and Jesus are terms that we can only use interchangeably, since the reality with which we are in communion is one and the same, and analysis of our experience, though on occasion it may disclose a difference of aspect, usually proves that the object of our worship would be falsely described if either God or Jesus were omitted.

The important points in considering the matter would seem to be two.

(1) If Jesus is indeed the unique expression for mankind of the nature of God, then as Christians we must not shrink from insisting upon the corollaries of our conviction. We must resist the tendency to treat God as different from Jesus or as manifesting Himself in spheres to which the revelation in Jesus does not apply. For example, the tendency to treat creation as a process that is actuated by motives and that displays values different from those of incarnation is in effect a

denial of the Godhead of Jesus. When we speak of God, for example, in relation to an earthquake or a bereavement, we must not do so in such a fashion as would make it inappropriate to replace the word God by the word Jesus. When we interpret the Old Testament or explain the Atonement, the character that we ascribe to God must be that which we see in Jesus. When we pray for the gift of the Holy Spirit or speak of the Spirit's work in inspiration or ordination, it is the Spirit of Jesus, and not some vague and magical influence, that we must have in mind. A casual examination of current theology or preaching will prove that God, far from being likened to our Lord, is too often credited with qualities of jealousy or injustice which would disgrace any decent human parent, that even among serious students the power behind the universe has never yet (save by the Fourth Evangelist) been seriously treated as Jesus " writ large."

(2) Although devotion to Jesus is wholly justified if He is worshipped as Son of God, the tendency to treat Him merely as " one of ourselves " and yet to love Him as a Saviour while refusing to recognise His cosmic significance, is close to idolatry. The type of piety crudely described as the " O dear Jesus " religion is an unpleasant perversion. The sentimental rhapsodies over certain scenes or phrases in the Gospels are hardly less repellent. Christianity is not a lonely love affair between me and Jesus. I cannot truly understand

or love Him unless I can see Him in my fellows, in mankind, in nature, in the world. He is God, not *a* God, God the eternal, not a patron saint or guardian angel peculiar to me and mine. Many of us, failing to make sense of the universe and despairing of God, fly by way of recompense to an ecstatic devotion to Jesus, just because He is not like reality, not like life, not like our fellows. He admits us to a refuge, a fairyland, where we can dream rosy dreams of our own exceeding preciousness and be sheltered from the rude world which shows so lamentable a lack of appreciation for us. It would be unchristian to treat such Jesus-worship with contempt : but it must be stated plainly that this is not Christianity nor indeed a wholesome form of religion. To isolate Jesus from God and then to worship Him is to fall into manifest inconsistency.

A final point may be briefly noticed.

(3) It is a common practice to separate the " Jesus of history " from the Jesus who has the cosmic value of God, and to use the title Christ to describe this latter aspect of His being. The objection to this otherwise convenient terminology is that it suggests and is often used to emphasise a vital distinction. Thus it is argued that the Jesus of the Synoptists was transformed by St. Paul and in Christian experience into the divine Christ, or even that Jesus was a mere prophet whom the ecstatic devotion of His followers deified and

worshipped. This seems to imply either that Jesus in the days of His flesh did not perfectly manifest the eternal values, or that His divinity depends not upon the quality but upon the scope of His manifestation. Believing as I do that the Synoptic portrait reveals the reality of God and that in this respect it is identical with the portrait in St. Paul or St. John, I cannot agree that the difference between His activity " in the flesh " and " in the Spirit " is any ground for assuming that in the one sphere He is " more divine " than in the other. The medium of revelation does not determine its value : and to me in both cases the value is that of God. To employ the term Christ would be to suggest a distinction in worth and nature as well as in scope and method. The eternal reality revealed through the medium of the human life of Jesus is the same as that which St. Paul and a multitude of Christians through the centuries have apprehended through their experience of the risen Jesus. Belief in the resurrection is not so much the belief in the empty tomb as the conviction that Jesus incarnate or cosmic, in body or in spirit, is one and the same, a continuous manifestation to those who know Him of the hidden things of God.

VIII

JESUS THE FIRST-FRUITS OF MANKIND

IF Jesus be, as we have maintained, divine, and divine both in His incarnate and in His risen life, is He not thereby cut off from the rest of mankind by a gulf so vast as to destroy any true identity between Him and us ? In making Him a legitimate object of worship, are we not destroying the value of His example ? Is the Incarnation anything but a drama in which the Son of God " veiled in flesh " assumed the form of servant and played His part on the stage of the world ? If this is admitted, then evidently His temptations are a " sham fight " ; His human nature is not really ours ; He starts at a different level and belongs to a different species. And our aspirations to be what He is, our claim that He is the first among many brethren, are mere presumption.

It must be recognised that the Church and especially certain Christian scholars and thinkers have often so emphasised the Godhead of Jesus as to reduce His manhood to the verge of unreality. Those to whom the Gospel was first preached were deeply influenced by conceptions of God which set the divine and the human in violent contrast. The

E

Jews of the time were definitely deistic : their sense
of the majesty of Yahweh had led them to isolate
Him from all direct contact with His creatures.
The Orientals held fast a dualism between spirit
and matter which made any idea of an incarnation
intolerable. The Greeks were sufficiently influenced
by the current philosophy as to define deity in
negative terms, contrasting the One with the many,
the Absolute with the relative, the immortal,
invisible, impassible, with the human. In a world
which regarded God and man as opposites, it was
natural that in asserting the Godhead of Jesus
Christians should minimise His manhood. And if
the tendency was strong in the early days it has
hardly grown weaker with the centuries. In Scripture the doctrines of the Fall and of the Virgin
Birth of Jesus gave warrant for maintaining that
He differed from us in kind rather than in degree.
In experience those who have felt the guilt of sin
and known the power of Jesus to save are naturally
led from the conviction that " only God could
redeem a man like me " to the conclusion that
mankind as sinners are wholly other than their
Saviour, totally estranged, save by His gift, from
any kinship with deity. Thus the very elements in
Jesus which differentiate Him from us become of
supreme value : we love to dwell upon the contrast between His worth and our nothingness : we
exalt Him by surrendering all claim to relationship
with Him. Pressed to its logical conclusion such
experience constrains us to deny all human merit, to

condemn all those who do not know and share the Christian faith, and to reduce the incarnation to a theophany.

Natural as it is for us to magnify the divine in Jesus, the result defeats its own purpose. To deny His manhood is to undermine the very foundation of the Christian religion. It is to bring us back into the mythologies with their stories of how gods once descended to earth and sojourned for a little while upon it. If Jesus is not very man in the same sense in which we are men, then He ceases to be the perfect translation of the eternal into terms of human life, and becomes a celestial invader whose triumphs do but mock us, and whom we are powerless to imitate and scarcely able to love or to understand. We cannot draw from His example any inferences as to our own nature : we cannot interpret Him by any analogies that we find in ourselves : He becomes unknown, inaccessible, alien, arbitrary.

Such a result, however strongly grounded in certain instincts of adoration and of humility, is in fact heretical as well as subversive. "The error," says Sir Henry Jones,[1] " does not spring from maintaining the divinity of Jesus but from denying the divinity of man." Starting from the non-Christian antithesis between God and man it builds upon a basis which in fact destroys all religion : if man has in him no affinity with

[1] Essay in *Jesus or Christ?* p. 101.

the divine, then all his efforts and aspirations are illusory : the gulf must ever remain unbridged, and we shall remain on the wrong side of it.

The case against it may be stated by a brief consideration (1) of Christian experience ; (2) of Christian doctrine.

(1) The contrast between God and man involves a conception of deity which lays stress upon the attributes of infinity and changelessness rather than upon the values of beauty, truth and goodness. Even so, to reject any relationship between God and ourselves would be to repudiate the experience of communion with the eternal to which mystics of all ages have made claim. If we can in any measure attain that knowledge of God which is eternal life, then there must be in us some element of affinity, some "spark of deity." And moreover, if our concepts of the eternal worth of beauty, truth and goodness are justifiable, they can only be so because in these respects we apprehend reality, and in pursuing them we are proving that the gulf can be crossed. Finally, if as Christians we believe that God is Love, and if we can see that love dimly in nature and manifestly in Jesus, then in so far as we are capable of love we are thereby at one with the divine, and God abides in us.

(2) Christian doctrine has always insisted not only that man was made in the image of God— that image which is Jesus Christ, but that there

is alike in the whole of creation and especially in humanity the Spirit of God, the "Power that worketh in us," and "whereby we cry Abba, Father." It is true that certain Churchmen have from time to time tried to restrict the operation of the Spirit to those who were admitted by baptism into the Christian Church—an attempt which is in conflict with Holy Scripture, with the Nicene Creed and with the evidence supplied, for example, by the lives of Quakers. It is true that others have recently identified the Holy Spirit with the "risen Christ," and thus would either confine Him to the Christian or so interpret the "risen Christ" as to associate Him with the pre-existent Logos rather than with the living Jesus. In the latter case they have warrant in the prologue of the Fourth Gospel where the Logos not the Spirit is regarded as the divine element in all men, and in the Greek theologians who ascribed to the Logos all the functions of the Spirit. But the wisdom of the identification remains open to grave objection. We shall examine this matter, which is largely one of terminology, hereafter. Suffice it now to notice that whether as Logos or as Spirit, the divine element in man, the potentiality for response to God, the basis of affinity with God, is maintained by Christian orthodoxy. There is that in us which is not wholly of earth, which arouses a perpetual unrest, which all our selfishness and sin cannot wholly eradicate or defile, which makes us by birthright children of heaven.

The whole history of religion and especially episodes like the controversy over free will between Augustine and Pelagius shows how difficult it is to give full emphasis alike to the majesty of God and to the responsibility of man. In their desire to safeguard the "otherness" of God and the "creaturehood" of man certain writers draw so sharp a line between the supernatural and the natural as in fact to advocate a definite dualism which if pressed to its logical conclusion makes a real incarnation impossible and threatens the postulates of religion. Others, as Dr. Oman[1] has so clearly proved, by treating divine grace mechanically or even chemically, fall into a dilemma from which determinism is the only escape. Yet others, anxious, as every practical worker must be, to stimulate the sense of human initiative, so exaggerate man's freedom as to make God rather an aid to our efforts than the sole source of all our aspirations. By its doctrine of the Holy Spirit, the divine in man, the Church can insist upon the reality of our affinity with God and avoid all complacency or reliance upon ourselves. We shall maintain at once the unique divinity of Jesus and His full Manhood. His relation to us will be that of the "perfect round" to the "broken arcs," of the white light to the myriad hues of the spectrum. Incarnation will differ from inspiration, but in degree not in kind. In Jesus will be the fullness of

[1] In *Grace and Personality*.

that Logos of which we by virtue of our humanity possess what Justin Martyr called " seeds." The perfect Man is for us men the incarnate Son of God : He could not be so unless we were in our measure also sons—prodigal sons—of the same Father.

IX

JESUS AND THE DOCTRINE OF THE TRINITY

It is a singular irony that the men who first strove to vindicate the unity of the Godhead revealed in nature, in Jesus and in the spiritual life of mankind should have formulated their work in a creed which has been generally used to emphasise not the unity but the distinctness of these modes of God's self-revelation. But the fate of the doctrine of the Trinity is a warning to all dogmatists. It was intended to be as lucid as human intellect could make it : it has been treated as a sanctified enigma. It was devised as a formula of peace : it has been a ceaseless cause of strife. It sought to repudiate tritheism : it is commonly supposed to sanction it. It was the result of a long period of enquiry : it has been divorced from its context and used in ways that would have horrified its authors. And the result is plainly to be seen. Dogmatic theology has fallen into disrepute : men who accept and advocate the claims of Jesus generally disclaim all wish to discuss the doctrinal explanation of them : and the fruit of three centuries of Christian experience and scholarship has become a butt for the wit of Mr. H. G. Wells.

Yet religion without doctrines is manifestly an impossibility if religion is ever to be described or proclaimed. We must have a theology of some sort, and it is not a matter of indifference whether it be sound or silly. Those who nowadays endorse the attitude of "Hang Theology Rogers" mean well: they wish to simplify the issues and get rid of speculative metaphysics: but indiscriminate denunciation does more harm than good. Indeed at present the revolt against the intellectual element in religion is one of the most serious obstacles in the way of revival. For if doctrinal principles are neglected, the substitute for them is either blind submission to arbitrarily chosen authorities or else the satisfaction of a popular and usually sentimental demand. "This is Catholic," or "This stimulates devotion," replaces "This is true." Recent controversies over the sacraments are due partially to the uncertainties of a time of transition but chiefly to the failure of the Church to formulate her theology in terms of the best knowledge of the time.

If she is to do so, it is not enough to accept the findings of the Œcumenical Councils as irreformable. They consisted of men singularly like ourselves, men of mixed motive and incomplete knowledge. They were held under the pressure of immediate needs, and often in an atmosphere of acute partisanship. Sycophancy and secular pressure, jealousies and ambition were not absent; indeed, in two out of the first four, were disgracefully obvious. The belief that a special providence dictated their findings or precluded them from error is mere superstition. God's revelation to them was conditioned as always by their power to receive it. Let all this be granted. Yet at the Council of Nicea, before political power had contaminated the great bishops and orthodoxy had become the prize of successful intrigue, great men debated a great issue, and formulated a result not unworthy of the long and patient labours of the noblest epoch in Church history. To brush aside their work as quibbling or as out of date is to confess oneself ignorant of the facts and unappreciative of intellectual worth.

During the formative period of its thought the Church was confronted with one supreme issue. Jesus and the deepest instinct of mankind rejected every sort of polytheism. " Hear, O Israel, the Lord thy God is one " was a creed universally accepted. Yet Jesus had been acclaimed as divine, and the whole experience of Christendom endorsed the claim. His immediate followers had spoken freely of God the Father, of His Son, Jesus Christ, and of the Holy Spirit, and though the Early Church hesitated in its interpretation of the formula, belief in the Trinity won its way to universal acceptance. How were these apparent contradictions to be resolved ? If God was one, who then was Jesus ? Between a monotheism which would reject His divinity and a polytheism which would degrade it, was there any middle way ?

THE DOCTRINE OF THE TRINITY

Logic might insist on the oneness of deity : experience would reply that if Jesus were not God then the Christian's faith was an illusion.

Two great men had prepared the way for the Creed. Tertullian, the Latin-speaking lawyer of Carthage, had supplied the terms " substance " and " person "—the latter of course meaning rather " rôle " or " party " than individual or person in the modern sense. Origen, the greatest mind of Greek Christianity, by insisting that the relationships of Father and Son were eternal, had cleared away the difficulties of the human analogy. Hosius and Athanasius, their representatives at Nicea, were not unworthy of their respective traditions. The result was the original form of the Nicene Creed.

Its purpose was clear. Arius had adopted the easy belief, which educated paganism could so freely accept, that, whereas God was in Himself unknowable, Jesus was His representative, not indeed truly God, nor yet wholly man, but the mediator between them. The Council's task was to insist that this was veiled polytheism, that God was one, whether as Creator or as Redeemer, that the three names, Father, Son and Spirit, represented not three divine Beings, but three eternal and co-existent modes of the one Godhead, that therefore Jesus was not a God or a demi-god, but the very God incarnate, and that in worshipping Him we were in communion with nothing less than deity. Arianism separated the Son from the

75

Father; the Creed united them, insisting twice over and in the plainest terms upon their essential unity.

It is one of the obvious difficulties in doctrinal study that men turn naturally to the categories of material objects or individual people for their definition of God, and that to Godhead neither category applies. The Greek Fathers previous to Nicea sought analogies to the Trinity from natural objects: the spring, its stream, its waves, or the sun, its radiance, its beams (which are close to Sabellianism or Unitarianism), or from cruder images—the boat-builder and the boat, the vine-dresser and the vine, which were ditheistic or Arian. Nicea itself was closer to the Sabellian than to the tritheistic position: it stresses the unity of substance, rather than the distinctness of persons. Half a century later when "person" ceased to mean "mode" or "aspect," and came nearer to its modern popular significance, we get the analogy of three men, Paul, Silas and Timothy; and this led easily to theories in which Father, Son and Spirit were sharply differentiated. Had the early Church been less influenced by physical metaphors, had it followed the Johannine doctrine of God as Love, Light, Life, the difficulties would have been much less acute. For the eternal Love, the source and stay of all creation, manifested to nature and man by the creative Word, and received by them in virtue of the indwelling in them of the Spirit which "makes for righteousness," is at once one and exists, or at least is known, under three eternal modes of His being.

God is not confined to or involved in the Universe: He is transcendent as well as immanent. To his transcendent Being, on which ultimately all else depends and from which all else proceeds, we may well give the name the Father. The universe appears to serve a purpose, to be constituted upon a plan: for mankind at least this purpose appears as an objective manifestation, as certain values to which we aspire, as a Word to which we give ear and obedience. Here is God forming, guiding, educating His creatures, God the Logos, God the Son, manifesting deity always, but supremely so with and in Jesus. And in creation itself there is a power which obeys and responds, a power acquiring ever fuller and richer expression as new levels of fulfilment emerge in the process of evolution. These " modes " are not mere activities of a single divine Being: each is personal though not individual— or so its quality and effects seem to demonstrate. Certainly it would be wholly inadequate to describe them as less than personal, though our experience of personality is so bound up with ideas of individuality and limitation that even personal seems hardly a sufficient description for life so dynamic and uncircumscribed. For myself I prefer the term " mode " as avoiding the idea of three Gods: but if " person " be stripped of all that denotes an individual or separate self, then the more familiar word may stand. In these days as at Nicea it is important to emphasise the unity of the Godhead. Did I not on Sunday last listen to a hymn in which were the lines :

> " And Jesus raised His languid eye
>   And met His Father's anger."

a hymn which is, alas ! only typical of much that passes for Protestant orthodoxy.

(*D*) MAN IN JESUS

X

IF Jesus is the sacrament of God, it is, as Canon Quick [1] has demonstrated, not sufficient that He be the expression of deity : He must also be its instrument, fulfilling the divine purpose. The doctrine of the incarnation is the Church's attempt to vindicate and explain her faith that Jesus is like God, His unique and adequate representative for mankind. As such it is supplemented by the doctrine of Atonement, which maintains and would rationalise the fact that Jesus accomplishes the object for which creation exists, that in Him we have not only access to but co-operation with the Father, that He is Saviour and Redeemer as well as Revealer. To contrast the two doctrines is absurd : to separate them is not easy ; for every expression is also an instrument. But to consider the atoning work of Jesus will be to supplement what has been already surveyed, and to discuss its application to our personal and corporate life.

The word Atonement has for many of us a

[1] *The Christian Sacraments*, pp. 55-100.

singularly repellent effect: our reaction to it is often almost one of disgust. For it has come down to us associated with ideas that outrage our instincts, ideas ugly and untrue and unworthy of the goodness of God, ideas derived from metaphors used in earlier times but now generally inappropriate. The chief of these are four—the metaphor of a sacrifice for sin, of a ransom paid to Satan, of a debt discharged to God, and of salvation from a hell of unending torment. All these can be supported, to some extent, by Scriptural phrases: all of them have the authority of great theologians of the past: and all of them produce in us a sense of repulsion.

Yet all of them have at one time or another commended themselves to men of real saintliness, and cannot be lightly set aside. Beneath them there lies some element of truth which we must not lose. A generation like our own, which is inclined to a rather easy optimism and often treats the love of God as a sentimental and not very moral amiability, must be very careful not to reject unexamined ideas which emphasise His " severity " alongside of His goodness. If there is no room for fear in religion, there is abundant need for awe. And indeed anyone who has passed beyond the superficial cheerfulness of the ignorant cannot but find in life much that terrifies. The road to peace leads through places of darkness and suffering, of penitence and utter humiliation. If we discover at last that " the wrath of God " is a misinterpretation of the Father's character, we shall yet confess with

a deepened conviction of its truth that we are
" children of disobedience."

The revolt against doctrines of the atonement
which represent it rather as a salvation from sin
than the attainment of eternal life has been influenced
by two unjustifiable ideas—an erroneous concept of
progress, and an exaggerated sense of helplessness :
on the one hand we " vaguely trust that somehow
good will be the final goal of ill," on the other we
feel ourselves in the grip of vast and soulless forces
that we cannot resist or overcome.

(1) We have seen so huge an enrichment of
man's material wealth, of his knowledge in every
department of physical and practical life, of his
civilisation and social order, that we jump to the
unjustified conclusion that thereby our real welfare
must needs be increased. It is always a temptation
to regard the world of sense-perception as more
real than that of the Spirit : men still speak as if a
" literal," by which they mean a material, Second
Advent were more actual than a Coming like that to
St. Paul on the Damascus road : and to slip from
this into the belief that we are necessarily less
sinful because we live more comfortably and have
a larger equipment of machinery is fatally easy.
We need to be reminded that the Kingdom of God
is not eating and drinking, Garden Cities, and
cinemas and aeroplanes and the wireless, and that
so far as these things distract our attention from the
real values of life, from love and joy and peace and

courage, from God, we may in fact be worse. Many of us would seem to be so occupied with the new amusements and the new stresses that we become blind to the selfishness of our own existence and insensitive to the sufferings of others. God is forgotten in our concern with " the things that are made." We trust the larger hope without consecrating ourselves to its fulfilment.

(2) And, moreover, when our consciences prick us and we turn uneasily in our sleep there is an excuse for sloth ready to hand. Biologists with their insistence upon heredity, economists with their talk of law, psychologists with their stress upon primitive instincts, have combined to make us feel helpless and enslaved. Sin is not our fault if we are the slaves of our ancestry or of circumstances or of our own subconsciousness. So we fall back upon the discussion of problems, throwing into the abstract and objective evils which we ought to see in our own selves. To condemn the world for its toleration of wrongs which of course we as individuals cannot remedy, is easier than to trace the roots of those same wrongs into our own souls and cure them there. To reform the world by the redistribution of other people's money, by the education of other people's children, by politics or by eugenics is far pleasanter than to reform ourselves. We need to be warned, as Professor Urwick has lately warned us, that " human society means Smith and me—and God ; just that

and nothing more ; human progress means making better the relations between Smith and me—and God ; and human good means the happiness which Smith and I may perhaps be able to find together, with the help of God." [1]

It may be argued that in any case it is better to be interested even in material things than to dismiss the world as a vale of tears and to denounce beauty as a snare of the devil, truth as " veiled infidelity," and love as " wilful condoning of wickedness " ; or that the discovery of corporate failure is a gain even if it weakens our sense of individual responsibility. But the plain fact is that we have recoiled from a sense of sin which was morbid and often an " inverted pharisaism," and from an idea of judgment which was vindictive and often self-righteous into the opposite error of denying sin and judgment in every form. And this is of course mere folly : for with the evidences around us and within of our personal and corporate failings and of their inevitable consequences in blood and tears none of us can honestly dispute our need for redemption.

Indeed the old account of sin and judgment, morbid as it was, erred on the side of insufficiency. It regarded sin as the commission of certain wrongful acts, the breaking of laws, the omission of duties : sins could be classified into mortal and venial : they could be forgiven in the sense that the actual error could be wiped out and the past be

[1] *The Social Good*, p. 2.

undone. And judgment was set in the future, as an event which should happen after death or at a great assize at the world's end, when a final verdict should be passed once for all and mankind irrevocably and arbitrarily classified into the saved and the damned. Such a belief was undoubtedly successful in inculcating the dread of hell into those who took it seriously : it gave an unpleasant doctrine of assurance to those who were satisfied of their own acquittal, and authorised them to anticipate the sentence which should overwhelm their less pious neighbours. Hence the type of Christian whose life was spent in—

> " Condoning sins that they're inclined to
> By damning those that they've no mind to,"

a type barely separable from the Pharisee.

Set against that the three facts which represent the attitude of to-day :

(1) Sin is separation from God : it is man's failure to realise the true values of existence, to live in accordance with God's will and the measure of the stature of Christ : it is selfishness, lack of love for God and man, the devoting to selfish ends of energies which can only grow as they are spent in sympathy and service : it is spiritual blindness and apathy, the acceptance of perverted standards, the ignoring of the eternal. Wrong action is only the symptom of a wrong state. The action is a crucifying of the innocent—always

and everywhere when I choose evil others suffer for it, first my nearest and dearest and then an ever-widening circle of my fellows : and the wrong state is my estrangement from God, expressing itself in a breaking of fellowship with my neighbours.

(2) Every sin brings its own judgment ; and the judgment is that I have done wrong and infected with evil the lives of others. Judgment is in process here and now. I reject God and am myself cut off by my own act from Him, sending myself into the hell which is loneliness and pride and contented acquiescence in failure and in the poisoning of others. There is no need for any judicial penalty over and above this inevitable result of my error.

(3) The past cannot be undone : the chain of consequences cannot be broken. I reap and others reap what I have sown. Penitence is the recognition of sin : forgiveness is re-union with God : salvation is the power to begin afresh as His child : redemption is the ability to learn by our failures and to bring good out of evil. But the scars remain. I may be the more glorious because of them, if I am enabled by them to escape from complacency and self-confidence. But others suffer for my faults and not all my tears can repair the harm that I have done to them. I have stoned the prophets, slain the Son of God ; and though I may then build their tombs and see Him rise from the dead, that

which I have done remains. If good comes out of evil, yet, as St. Paul is always insisting, I am not thereby justified in evil-doing.

Our recognition of evil and our power to rise from it depend solely upon our vision and understanding of God. If He is what Jesus is, and if we have in us the capacity to respond to Him, then a real oneness, a true atonement, is possible ; and Jesus, who has revealed the kinship of God and man and enabled us to fulfil the realities of our true nature, is Himself the sole instrument of that atonement. To express the perfect image of God, to initiate the era of life in God, to reveal God in us—it was for this that He gave Himself to be crucified. It is sacrifice, complete and sufficient ; ransom to set us free from the bondage of selfishness and lovelessness ; redemption that we may dwell in God, and God in us ; salvation that here and now we may know ourselves to be in heaven and possessed of eternal life. Realising itself as the body of the incarnate deity, mankind is made at one. There are no conditions except that we believe the good news: " Ye being many are one body in Christ, and severally members one of another."

XI

OUR LIFE IN JESUS

THE mode of the Atonement is so simple that only those who get entangled by metaphors can miss its secret. It is because the evil that I do flows into others and infects them that I cannot bear the consequences of my sin alone; and it is by the same influence of person upon person that I am saved. There is only one alchemy that has the magical power of transmuting the clay of my life into gold, only one spell that can raise me from the dead; and that is the love of one who knows me through and through and yet loves me, of one who can call out all that remains of decent feeling in me and kindle the spark into a flame of devotion. We become what we love: that is an elementary law of growth. If I fill my mind with lust and greed, I become lecherous and a glutton: if I can see no object more attractive than myself, my fate is that of Narcissus, to be stifled by my own image. Every friend that I make leaves his mark upon me for better or worse; there is something in me that is not mine but his. And those who evoke and satisfy my whole self transform me into their likeness. So Jesus, when I see

Him " lifted up," draws me, possesses me, recreates me. His nearest disciples have known that His Spirit was their spirit, that they had His mind, that " they lived, yet not they ; Christ lived in them." For such it was no metaphor but sober and literal fact to say that they were His body. They were at one with God because one with Christ.

Here as always the Christian scheme is simple and natural. Its meaning is only lost or concealed when the Crucifixion is separated from its consequents. Doctrines of Atonement, in their anxiety to keep the supremacy of the Cross, often distort the facts by representing the death of Jesus as by itself, and apart from its effect on us, efficacious : thence follow all the insincerities and mythologising that have gathered round the words " substitution," " transaction," " justification "—insincerities which involve God in a partnership of fraud and enable men to account themselves righteous. The Cross is indeed the dramatic act by which man's estrangement and need are revealed and met : there he discovers the love of God, there God reconciles His lost child to Himself. But that is only the beginning. Love is born in the passion and ecstasy of self-surrender : but as every lover knows it may easily die young. What starts as an emotional outbreak must be tested intellectually : we must learn what Jesus is, and face the enormous difficulties of accepting Him as a reasonable interpreter of God, else our faith will never grow up, but will always be at the mercy of moments of scepticism and apathy. Only when feeling and mind are alike convinced can love be tried out and confirmed in action, in the daily round of life. It is as we discover Jesus to be not only the Way of access to God, but the Truth about reality, and the Life which is eternal, that our union with Him becomes a possession for ever, part and parcel of our very selves, permeating and changing the whole quality of our being. And at every stage, as we know only too well, we can slip away from Him and forget and deny; and always too we can discover fresh contacts and a deeper comradeship and a more devoted discipleship, as He dominates more and more our whole sky.

As such love influences us it sets us free for growth, free alike from the desire for low and selfish gratification and from the limitations of complacency, of ignorance, of weakness of will. Its effect is an immense vivifying of our emotional life which takes on fresh richness of tone, a finer appreciation, a quicker sensibility. Ugliness of every kind begins to distress us : we instinctively reject it : for we have discovered a beauty which makes the lusts of the flesh and the excitement of the senses seem gross and unworthy. And on our minds it has a similar result : as we adjust our ideas to our new experience of God we realise how scrappy and incomplete has been our philosophy of life, how inconsistent our principles, how irrational our behaviour: we begin to think straight, to understand the meaning of life, to range our thoughts in order; to detect inconsistencies and sophisms, to strip our minds of cant, to prove all things by their conformity with our new knowledge of God. Upon our wills the consequences are still more plain: we no longer fight a losing battle against evil, building up its hold upon us by the energy of our attempts to repress it: we no longer want to go wrong, are no longer fretted by inward conflict: our instincts are sublimated and our personalities integrated: we experience what St. Augustine called " the blessed necessity of not sinning ": our wills are free because they are no longer our own, and enslaved, but God's.

The vitalising power of such love, as we see it in the Christianity of the Catacombs or of St. Francis, or of many a simple, saintly soul to-day, is in striking contrast with what is commonly accounted religious. Too often the Church is supposed to stand for a type of character morbidly introspective, rigidly disciplined, meticulously observant of ecclesiastical rules, easily shocked by natural gaiety, sternly critical of all worldly concerns, achieving at best a negative virtue that is more unlovable than vice, and at worst the affected self-righteousness of the " unco' guid." Every parson knows how prevalent this impression is by the attitude which ordinary folks are apt to assume towards him: they " bridle " or " bristle " at sight of the collar ; get on the defensive ; assume a mask of propriety, of piety, or of apology : he feels that his presence is rather depressing than exhilarating, that the temperature is chilled and the conversation strained. This is precisely the reverse of what ought to be if God is indeed Light and Life and Love. And the cause of it is that Christianity, and especially its doctrine of Atonement, has been for so long associated with joyless services, with an obsession about sin, with other-worldliness and fear of judgment, with priest-craft and little books of self-examination, with duties rather than joy, restraints rather than adventure.

If Atonement means love, and if God is like Jesus, then plainly the Christian will be one who is only ascetic in so far as all art involves and achieves a certain purity of soul, who is sympathetic with every disinterested quest for knowledge, who is distressed by the fact of sin just because it means separation from God. He will rejoice in men for what they are and still more for what they have it in them to be. Nothing will be common or unclean, though everything save Jesus will be incomplete, and much will be tragic and agonising. Everywhere he will recognise some real worth, some thwarted but persistent urge towards full and abounding life, some evidence of native godliness. He will be looking upwards, and outwards, and forwards—" unto Jesus "—rather than downwards toward sin, or inwards at his own processes, or backwards to the past and its traditions. And in his soul will be the fortitude that is born of suffering, and the peace that comes from inward unity, and the joy of one who has lost his life and found it, and the love which only God in Christ Jesus can inspire and satisfy.

And if such an account seems idealistic or extravagant, it relates only to an end and to means which the New Psychology is accentuating. Despite the morbid tendencies of some of its exponents and the occasional exaggeration of its analytical methods, the positive contribution of psychologists and psychotherapists has been to emphasise the two facts : first, that integration or unifying of personality is accompanied by an enormous enhancement of vitality and power ; and secondly, that such integration is achieved as the person comes under the influence of a motive strong enough to attract and dominate his interest. Without necessarily agreeing with Freud and his followers in ascribing a sexual origin to all personal relationships, we may claim their support for the conviction that love is the master-motive in human life, and that for a complete development of personality love, if directed towards a worthy object, can accomplish a sublimation otherwise unattainable. We may even go further and claim that psychologists, in setting before us the goal of self-realisation, in so far as they mean by this that we should become our own highest selves, are only saying that we must rise to the level of the divine element in us, to the measure of the fullness of the stature of Christ, of " the Christ in us the hope of glory." If Jesus is the perfection of our own true manhood, then to reach our own fulfilment is to live in Him. And love, not self-conscious imitation, is the way to such life.

We cannot gain this life by perpetual contemplation of our own faults or of our own merits, by the elaborate business of " taking thought," which the Confessional too often encourages and Jesus always forbids. Healthy organisms are concerned with their ends, not with their processes. As we learn to see Him in Himself and in His world, we shall have little time to bother about anything of less importance. Neither the fear of a future hell nor the hope of a future heaven will enter our minds : we have Him here and now, and nothing matters except that we so often lose Him. Even then, when selfishness leads us into denying Him, and pride makes us blind to His likeness in our fellows, what hurts most is not the effect of sin on ourselves but our failure in love. We shall suffer as every one suffers who betrays his friend or disgraces his family, suffer for having preferred starvation and husks to our home : but it will be the Father rather than our own self-pity or discomfort that will draw us back again. And we shall know that His welcome is sure and free. Repentance means for the Christian what it meant on the lips of Jesus, " Believe the good news," not what the Baptist expressed by it, " Recognise your sins and get rid of them." No doubt the turning round of the personality from self to God can be described in either fashion : it is both an escape from sin and a discovery of love. But psychologically and practically it makes all the difference whether our interest is in what we desire to overcome or in what we see of the eternal, in our own diseases or in the health of heaven. We shall never live as simply and naturally and unself-consciously in God as we do in our own homes, we shall never accept the love of Jesus as freely as a child accepts the love of its mother, if we are constantly fretted with fears and ambitions, as though such life was not a fact to be enjoyed but a possession to be bought, as though such love were the reward of our merits or a subject for our bargaining.

Moreover, it is only as we experience the reality of the good news that we shall appreciate the shame and folly of our own sin. The wonder of the love of God leaves us with no illusions about evil : we see it in ourselves as a blasphemy against beauty, a lie against truth, an outrage against friendship : we see it and are humbled to the dust. In me certainly dwelleth no good thing : I am blind and false and selfish, ready to exploit even my religion in the interests of my self-respect, quick to fortify my conceit by defaming others, drugging my conscience by a meticulous absorption in duties, living by rote and rule. That is I am living " under law," even, as St. Paul would say, " under sin," not under grace and in liberty. Yet to cry with him " Wretched man that I am, who shall rescue me from this state of death," is also to cry, "I thank God through Jesus Christ, my Lord." For the death of self involves a burial—and a resurrection.

XII

OUR FELLOWSHIP IN JESUS

It is of the new life of the Christian that the Apostle writes " All things are yours; for ye are Christ's and Christ is God's." To be at one with Jesus is to discover Him everywhere and in Him the whole world. The meek possess the earth : that is a fact of common experience. As we cease to be preoccupied with ourselves we have room for other and more interesting objects of contemplation : our sympathies increase and their range expands. Any sudden liberation from self effects a change almost miraculous. We see the world as if at that moment it had been newly created : common things take on novelty ; familiar scenes become romantic ; dull people disclose themselves as full of worth ; we understand, and pardon or admire. Every lover lives in fairyland, and though when the first freshness fades he is apt to think that the glamour has departed and even to try artificial stimulants to renew it, in fact if he is patient and faithful he can then gain that which nothing can take away.

The trouble about our human loves is that they so often become exhausted. We reach the limit of our friend's capacity to surprise and enchant us: he becomes a second self and the pair of us succumb to selfishness *à deux*; or he fails to grow with us or ahead of us, and there is a slow or speedy disillusionment. In real love there is always an element of mystery, a something unexpected and undiscovered, a perpetual surprise. New situations are always revealing new growth: the relationship is always the same and yet never stale, for it is always being adjusted to a fresh environment, and each change of scene involves the excitement of an adventure into the unknown. This is of course the whole secret of the art of living, that having discovered the eternal we have yet the endless joy and wonder of finding wider manifestations of it, of exploring contact with it in every sort of setting. Just as the innermost reality presents itself to us through an infinitely graded series of semblances which are each in their measure its sacramental expressions and instruments, so the eternal enters into our experience through a myriad happenings in time, by which we have communion with the timeless. History not less than nature is the sacrament of God, the outward sign of His inward Spirit.

It is this sense at once of peace and movement, of underlying permanence and yet perpetual discovery, that gave to the early Christians their characteristic quality of joy. God stood firm: neither life nor death could shake the stability of His love and their trust. Yet in every phase of their sojourn on earth they could explore new aspects of His nature and discover new evidence of His presence. And that presence gave to the world an ever fresh worth and interest. Suffering was welcome because in it they found a deeper understanding of God; pain and danger only helped them to share the passion of Jesus; death was the prelude to a still closer communion. And all the beautiful and ordered life of earth was radiant with His light, a reflection of His unearthly glory. None could be dull or depressed or lonely in such a home with such a comradeship. The sin and misery of the world around them, their own weaknesses and failures, aroused an agony of compassion and stimulated a heroism of effort. They existed not to contemplate but to serve, not for a blessed idleness but for an enthusiasm of redemptive activity. The darkness in which they were set bade them kindle their lamps and lift them high, to seek the lost and share with them the light. With a serious gaiety like that of a child playing a game that demands all its attention and yet is only a game, they threw themselves into their venture for God. And with them was Jesus, their Orpheus, drawing to Him all creation, stones and trees and beasts and men, by His music, bringing the dead to life and renewing the youth of the world.

From the first the strength and glory of life in Jesus were that it was the common possession of a fellowship, that the disciple was not alone but one of a family. It was to the body of believers that the gift of Pentecost had come : the blessed community was the first and chief result of the gift. Men and women who had been brought one by one into the company of Jesus, after they had passed under the liberating spell of His love, found themselves welded together and incorporated into a single organism.

It is a familiar fact that those who have shared a great experience and been inspired by a common loyalty manifest what is usually called a "group personality." We need not here enter into the difficult problem as to whether a "group mind" is or is not an entity other than the minds that compose it. But at least it is certain that under conditions of intimacy and in response to a common ideal men find themselves so sensitive to one another and so integrated by the same motive that they act as if under the control of a single will. In the jargon of the day, when several units "come together" in this fashion and under these conditions, there is the "emergence" of something new. No doubt there is nothing in the group which is not in the members, just as in a quartz crystal there is nothing but the molecules of silicon dioxide; yet both group and crystal emerge as novelties differing in quality from that which composes them.

Quite evidently the fellowship of the early Church was of this order, and rightly described as "the body of Christ." There was singularly little of individualism in its religion. The special talents of any particular member were valued by him and by his fellows because they enriched the

life of the society : his efforts were directed not
to the saving of his own soul but to the building-up
of the body : his failures and successes affected
others as much as himself : he was not alone, but
always held up by obligation and encouraged by
sympathy. St. Paul had in him a large measure
of individualism ; by nature and opportunity he
was a pioneer, exploring new territory and refusing to build on another man's foundation. Yet
always his loneliest exploit aims not at his own
development but at the welfare of the Church,
and as he grows older more and more does he
test his decisions by the effect that they will have
upon his brethren. He finds the Spirit of Christ
not in the isolation of his own mystic experience
so much as in the corporate life of the body in which
Christ again dwells.

This sensitiveness to the common good, this
response to the mind of the fellowship, gave to the
Church unity but not uniformity. Only in later
ages, when the first spontaneous co-operation had
been replaced by a rigid discipline of regulations,
did the Christians begin to adopt the method and
spirit of an organisation. An army cannot encour-
age originality : its soldiers must march in step
and be drilled in simultaneous and standardised
actions : freedom is forbidden : all must be
modelled upon the same pattern. In the interests
of efficiency, as we can see from a study of Church
history, a strong case can be made for the mechan-
isation of activities. Natural growth is apt to be

turbulent and disorderly : surely its exuberance must be pruned and its new branches trained : we cannot trust the tree to achieve symmetry unaided. Gardening is a precious art. St. Paul himself would claim the duty of fostering and if need be checking the development of the seeds of the Spirit. But when horticulture becomes over-elaborate it too often prefers the artificial and the distorted, and the plant is so lopped and tied, so over-stimulated in one direction and atrophied in another that its vitality is impaired and its beauty debased into monstrosity. Religion can be helped by wise and loving organisation : but the dangers of arbitrary interference with natural processes are not negligible. And in the case of the Church too often a living fellowship has been organised into a moribund institution. Indeed the miracle of Christendom is nowhere more clearly seen than in the fact that its vital principle has survived so many centuries of effort to regulate and restrict it. The inner and eternal life, pent up by legalism, regimented by the hierarchy, conventionalised in the interests of safety and mechanised for the sake of efficiency, retains its power of breaking out explosively in fresh and most disconcerting direc-tions. The organism has not yet been successfully transformed into an organisation.

And where the real experience of living eternally in Jesus is shared by the fellowship of believers its power is still Pentecostal. And that in two directions.

(1) For the individual, membership in such a group lifts a casual and spasmodic communion with Jesus into an abiding and constraining assurance of His presence. The lonely soul has its glimpses of heaven : there are moments of infinite sweetness when it is indeed in the Lord. But such discipleship is too often dependent upon circumstance and temperament, and has to contend against the perils of complacency and of despair. I am tempted either to live for my great moments, deliberately neglecting for their sake the plain duties of the common day and isolating them from the rest of my existence, or to regard them as an illusion, created by my instincts in order to reconcile me to the bleak dulness and bitter futility of life, a coward's refuge, a school-girl's day-dream. Individualistic religion too easily degenerates into a fantasy in which this mean and stunted self can masquerade in a wonderland of colour and warmth, and gain a fictitious sense of its own dignity and power.

(2) From whatever experience it starts, the love of God grows by discovering fresh manifestations of His presence in an ever-widening field. We cannot love God without at the same time loving our brethren. But to look on them with sympathy, to recognise them as " in the family," is not the same as sharing in their love and being welcomed by them as a brother. To be one of a group means that we have tested and found true our vision of

the brotherhood of mankind. Seeing Jesus we
have been convinced of the divine possibilities of
humanity ; we have felt that the blessed community
was no mere ideal and our whole selves have been
aglow with trust and friendliness. Sharing our
discipleship with others we transmute our faith
into fact. Here is the community already in being :
its life flows over into us : we are caught up into it,
sustained and energised by it : in it we are at home.
The relationship thus discovered is independent
of our temperament or condition : we are in the
Kingdom not as lonely sojourners but as native
to its soil and akin to its folk. We may deny our
birthright by our failure to live worthily of it :
we cannot annul or forego it : these others have
claims upon us, and will not let us go. Wherever
we wander, their love goes with us and suffers
and recalls us. And more and more we are aware
that our life is one with theirs—and God's.

(*E*) ETERNAL LIFE

XIII

JESUS AND THE CHURCH

RELIGION involves myself and God and the fellow-ship.

A church of some sort is an essential; for there is no such thing, outside an asylum, as the completely isolated individual, and religious experience demands and creates the society of believers. Nor can the Church dispense with outward ordinances, with continuity of witness, with some sort of co-ordination, with differences of status and duty. It has been called a body and in a body there are many members differing in office though not in honour. As the organism's range of activities increase and its adjustment to a widening environment becomes more complex, there is constant need for fresh and specialised functions: we must recognise the process for what it is, the growth of the Church of Jesus. We can distinguish two main phases of this growth in the past and are now entering upon a third.

(1) The original fellowship of Pentecost was during the centuries evolved into a society equipped

with an apparatus of doctrine, order and ceremonial, with control vested in the hierarchy, with special organs for educational, missionary, devotional and ascetic service, with power to locate and expel from the body agents hostile to its health. No doubt freedom of expansion was lost as development proceeded along definite lines; growth was not always symmetrical or harmonious and was often in directions which were not in the long run beneficial. Some critics would suggest that, in encasing itself with an armour of formularies, the Church followed the example of the Crustaceans and for the sake of a temporary security encumbered itself within a shell from which it can never break out, and that it is now safely imprisoned in a *cul-de-sac*. Certainly no student of biology would maintain that the organs necessary at certain stages of evolution were irreformable : if life can fashion an Archæopteryx out of a reptile or transform gill-slits into eustachian tubes, the living Church may well restate its creeds or replace a monarchical by a democratic system of government. But on the whole, even through its most difficult phases, there was growth of an orderly and consistent type such as to enable the survival of the organism in spite of the changes of its environment.

(2) Then when the unitary ideas of the Middle Ages gave way before the pressure of national and individual aspiration, the Church itself followed the destiny of the Empire, and split up into a

variety of communions capable, as the unified society was not, of meeting the religious needs and the newly-awakened consciousness of men and nations struggling for liberty and for the right to develop their own gifts. A strong and centralised organisation had protected the Church during the dark ages and given discipline and order to the mediæval era. Now the times had changed: a multitude of adventurers were exploring new knowledge and the New World, and had broken away from the limits of a system of belief and practice no longer adequate to express the wider life. We may regret that the outward unity of the Church was sacrificed and that reform took so violent a course. But we must recognise that the printing-press was in fact a more effective means of union than the Pope, and that the new groups or churches both enlarged and enriched the spiritual life of mankind. Here as before mistakes were made : there was complacent obscurantism as well as reckless experiment : men emphasised outward conformity so strongly as to suggest that they confused means with ends, and insisted upon membership in an organisation rather than upon spiritual vitality. Tests of orthodoxy and traditional ordinances had been useful in their day : no wonder that they were wrongly regarded as indispensable. Some reformers merely substituted the Bible for the Church and one set of regulations for another, while others, aware of the failure of the old system, were impatient of all restrictions,

JESUS AND THE CHURCH

and unable to see virtue in institutions of any kind. But on the whole the change was vastly to the good, a true expression of the energy of the Spirit of God; and the new churches have in the course of history shown themselves rich in the fruit of that Spirit.

It is obvious that the claim of any group or denomination to be reckoned as within the Church can only be tested by the reality of its union with God in Christ: so far as it is in living contact with Him, carrying on His work and displaying His power, it is His. No external sign or rite can of itself make a man or a society Christian: spiritual life cannot be magically imparted to us in spite of ourselves: we must receive and respond to God, and neither He nor His Church can compel us to do so. Nor can the lack of outward sign exclude or unchurch us: "Those that are led by the Spirit of God, they are the Sons of God." The criteria of Churchmanship are what Jesus described as the fruits of the good tree, the character and conduct that spring from love for God and man. The Church, in the true sense of the word, consists of all those who are in any way expressions or instruments of Jesus. So defined, the Church and the Kingdom of God are one and the same; and no man dare set bounds to their membership. For it is plain that multitudes of simple folk who know nothing about institutional religion, and of heroic souls who have " denied Christ for Christ's sake," are full of the authentic power of His Spirit. And those who talk of the Body of Christ cannot identify it with anything less. To apply so great a title to our own denomination alone is a piece of hypocrisy and of impertinence.

(3) Yet if the Church is the blessed company of all faithful people, what of the institutions, Roman or Anglican, Presbyterian or Congregationalist, Baptist, Methodist or Quaker, which commonly claim the title? It was, as we have suggested, a natural and by no means deplorable consequence of the Renaissance that the new interpretation of Christianity took for its expression very various forms of doctrine, ritual and order. The notion that all nations and peoples can find their capacity for worship fully satisfied by the Mass in Latin has only to be stated in order to be rejected. As well suppose that all English Christians will some day join the Salvation Army. God speaks to some through the Confessional and the *Sursum Corda*, to others through a Brass Band and the Testimony Meeting—to each according to his ability. And while men differ in talents, in race and culture, in language and temperament, " churches " ministering to their peculiarities will have a function to fulfil in the divine economy. No doubt as civilisation becomes international and as education diminishes the differences between individuals, the varieties of doctrine and cults will be lessened. No doubt even now some of them are becoming unnecessary. Certainly there are at present in

Britain tendencies both towards the assimilation of one type of worship to another and towards a richer elasticity within the denominational norms. We may legitimately feel that one " church " is on the whole nearer to the ideal than another. Even if at present diversity is desirable this does not mean that all forms are equally valuable : nor though their importance is secondary is it on that account negligible. As the denominations come together in asserting their fundamental unity in Christ, they will be able to discover and compare the merits of their respective methods not only of worship or doctrine, but of organisation and government. Gradually, and by a process partly of selection by survival and partly of deliberate reform, we shall reach a new synthesis in which the characteristic contributions of the separated bodies will be combined.

It is, for example, already plain that in Anglicanism the old monarchy of the bishop is giving place to a system in which the bishop becomes what he was originally, a presiding elder ; and that the development of moderators and of a secretariat in the non-episcopal bodies is giving to them a government not far from that of a constitutional episcopate. So too in doctrine, as the old ideas of infallibility are abandoned, there is revealed a very close consensus between theologians of all the protestant denominations—a consensus which binds together Anglican and Presbyterian, Congregationalist and Methodist, who share the new knowledge, far more closely than each is bound to the old-fashioned or obscurantist members of his own denomination. Similarly in church services the Puritan dislike of art and music is disappearing ; denominations with a fixed liturgy are making room for free and extempore prayer and for periods of silence, while many Free Churches are adopting forms of devotion based upon Anglican models. The excellent custom of holding united services or of interchanging pulpits enables ministers to pool their experience and make trial of unfamiliar modes of devotion ; and the result is an enrichment of their means for expressing and fulfilling their vocation. The Church of the future will no doubt have a normal system, a system that has emerged from the period of sectional experiment. It will also have very great freedom in trying fresh developments and in permitting a wide range of departures from the type.

For if it once be granted that the Church consists of those in whom is the Spirit, then the idea that its criteria can be fixed by outward signs, by pedigree or mode of organisation, by forms of doctrine or liturgy becomes absurd. If God comes to me in a Quaker meeting-house or a Baptist tabernacle, as He has in fact come, this means that through the outward signs or sacraments employed by those bodies God's inward life is bestowed. To talk about covenanted and uncovenanted mercies is to treat the Eternal as if He were a pettifogging attorney : to deny the " Churchmanship " of the

When we have explored the significance of Pentecost and in the little company of our fellow-worship-
pers have experienced the power of the Spirit of
Jesus, we may be equipped for wider ranges of
discipleship.

Eternal life has its source in the glowing splendour
of union with Jesus : it involves a similar union
with Him as I find Him in my fellows : some day
I shall learn to find Him everywhere. " The love
of the one leads on to the love of two, the love of
many leads on to the love of all." And if ideally
the Church includes all who are in God, it is
through the churches, through the groups and
denominations that constitute Christendom, that
each of us is trained for so universal a brotherhood.

XIV

RELIGION is communion between man and God:
for those to whom God is expressed by Jesus
such communion is quickened into love: always
it is a relationship, and can be considered from the
side of each party. We may describe it as a revelation or gift of Himself by God to man : that is true,
but if we accept it as the whole truth we plunge
into Calvinism. Or we may emphasise man's
response, his aspiration and worship ; and this too
is true, although by itself it is woefully incomplete.
At different epochs in Church history one or other
aspect has been exaggerated. God's grace can be
so stressed as to make man passive and powerless,
a puppet at the disposal of the Almighty. Or, as
is the fashion at present, man's temperament, his
suggestibility and visualising, can loom so large
as to reduce God to a mere projection or fantasy.
Between Augustine and Pelagius, and their succes-
sors down the ages, the pendulum swings. Each
extreme destroys the reciprocal character of the
religious experience, and in so doing fails to cover
the whole of the facts. God is not an illusion:
and I am not a marionette.

THE RESOURCES OF PRAYER

Eternal life viewed from its human side is usually summed up in the word " prayer." No other single term so fitly describes the relationship of the believer to God and to his fellows ; for prayer includes both worship and intercession, both communion and fellowship. " Pray without ceasing " is the Christian version of Aristotle's " So far as is possible live immortally."

To say so is to point out the inadequacy of the common idea of prayer, and to suggest a solution of the difficulties which usually beset those who discuss it. These mistaken concepts of prayer are two-fold : and each is very widely held.

(1) Prayer is often identified with the business of asking. We pray for particular things or people, for purity, for success, for the restoration of a friend to health, for foreign missions, for fine weather. And we reinforce our faith in the virtue of such petitions by collecting instances in which they appear to have been answered. It is difficult not to feel that such an idea treats God as if He were a Universal Provider with a large but rather casual mailing department for goods on order. Certainly many sermons on the subject suggest that His cistern of grace is waiting to flood our lives with blessings until we turn on the appropriate tap. Such metaphors no doubt can be construed into something like a half-truth. The trouble about them is that they " make of God a tame confederate, purveyor to our appetites " ; and of ourselves

mere "daughters of the horse-leech, crying Give, give." Incidentally of course they leave out the whole element of worship, and all that is involved in the clause which must govern all petition, " Thy will, not mine, be done."

(2) In reaction from this notion that we demand and God supplies is the idea that prayer is valuable merely for its "uplifting" effect upon ourselves. God may or may not exist: He may or may not listen: we cannot expect that He will alter for our sakes the chain of cause and effect, change the course of a disease or deflect the flight of a bullet. But nothing is more suited as a support to our own morale than prayer, nothing has a stronger power of suggestion: we at least are the better for it. "God be with me"; "Christ sustain me"; "Father, forgive me" are pleasantly sounding versions of "Every day and in every way I get better and better and better," even if really their meaning and efficacy are exactly the same. Why not dress up M. Coué's formula, which after all has been tried and proved potent, in a religious garb? It cannot do any harm, and of course if there is anything in the idea of a God, so much the better. Here again we have another type of metaphor, another and an equally inadequate half-truth.

That these two notions are vastly prevalent, even among religious people, will hardly be disputed. In case it be, consider the instance supplied during the Great War. The politicians who begged us to mobilise the prayers of the nation and the soldiers or sailors who said that we should only win when the nation was on its knees before God were not, I fancy, insincere. At any rate their appeals were quoted as evidence of deep religious feeling. Yet what did they imply? Certainly not that the nation should consecrate itself to see God and worship Him : for if it had done so, it would almost certainly have demanded an immediate peace or even have refused to fight. No : " prayer" to them was the English synonym for " the will to victory " : it was either a means of getting from God the fulfilment of our desires, or a mode of reinforcing our own determination to win. Self, not God, is the source and centre of the whole effort.

So crude an illustration may do less than justice to the worth of such an activity. The cry of the mother for her child's welfare, the wrestling of a young man against sexual temptation, the pleading of the sufferer for release from pain, these are petitions natural, human and most pathetic. But in so far as they are just the utterance of our need, in so far as they leave out God or treat Him merely as a name, they are not in any real sense prayer. For all prayer consists of the deliberate endeavour to set ourselves in communion with God and to realise and share His will. And as such our first task when we pray is to forget and escape from ourselves and our selfish desires.

What then is prayer?

The simplest illustration of it is perhaps that supplied by the prophet or poet. Such an one sees God; that is his primary function: and inspired by his vision he can give it such expression as will transmit its power to mankind. We hear or read, and there passes to us something of that which the prophet received. He opens up for us a new avenue into reality. He is indeed an intercessor, mediating between man and God. So in prayer, the first movement is Godward. Emptied of ourselves we adore Him: His Spirit enfolds us, possessing us as love alone can possess. And like the prophet we can pass on that which we receive. Holding fast our communion with God we can, so to say, reach out towards others, letting our influence or rather the divine influence that possesses us flow out to them. We shall not dictate what we think that they want: we shall probably not express our thought in words at all: we shall be conscious only of God's love for them and their need for Him: through us thus freed from selfishness God acts; and His action is as real and effective as if it were expressed through the prophet's utterance, is indeed more direct and immediate.

For, that the analogy between the spoken and the unspoken message is valid seems, to me at least, so probable as to be well-nigh certain. It is not only that the evidence for thought-transference and even for telepathy is very strong: no one, as

Dr. Streeter [1] has pointed out, can study the records of psychic research without being driven to admit its existence. But in common experience the influence of person upon person indicates that beyond the contacts established by the senses lie ranges of communication that are not confined to sight and hearing, touch or taste or smell. It is certain that the specialised sense-organs have been evolved out of a generalised sensibility, that in insects, birds and mammals this " protopathic " sensitiveness has not been lost, and that in mankind there is a mass of evidence pointing to its continued existence. Far from being affected only by the impressions that come to us through the senses we are subject to influences far more subtle and intimate. Thought no less than speech is an energy of the personality; we may not yet be able to measure it in terms of the calories expended or of the wave-length of the vibrations set in motion; but to deny its activity or to maintain that it can have no effect would be to fly in the face both of evidence and of reason.

And if my will expressed in thought and desire exerts real power, then the same is true of my will when dominated by and in harmony with God. All of us have experienced the divine infection as we have caught it from some Spirit-possessed friend : we have been aware that it was not with him but with God that we were in communion :

[1] *Reality*, pp. 293-9.

through him has come to us the very presence of his Lord. It is no illusion, but a fact of common experience that religion is caught rather than taught, and that we catch it from those who possess and are possessed by it, those whose lives are hid with Christ in God and who bear about with them the Spirit of Jesus. Each one of us has it in him to become a mirror of the eternal. If we keep clean the glass of our souls and turn it up to the light of God, we can reflect the light and pass on to others its radiance; and they will receive from us not ourselves but God. So to reflect and transmit God is prayer. It is our calling to pray without ceasing, to be children of light, mirrors of Him who lighteneth every man, candles of the Lord. And over that light neither darkness nor distance prevails.

XV

THE ADVENTURE OF SERVICE

PRAYER, the communion of the worshipper with
God and his fellows, has its consummation not
in ecstasy or quietism but in service and an abounding activity of redemptive effort. Over religion
has hung the influence of the East, the influence
which finds God in withdrawal from the world of
space and time, of nature and history, and makes
contemplation the means and Nirvana, or the
Beatific Vision, the end for the true life of man.
To contrast the spiritual with the material, the
timeless with the changing, reality with the sem-
blance of things and events is easy and to the
devout fatally attractive. Let us get away from
the ebb and flow, the stress and strain of the world ;
let us strip ourselves of all that binds us to our
earthly environment ; and then, swooning into the
arms of the infinite, let us enjoy the utter peace
which comes to those who have passed beyond
fear or desire, thought or effort. Surely this is that
losing of life which is life indeed.

No one who sees the hideous tragedy of those
who are bound fast upon the wheel of things, those
whose aim seems only to be comfort and prosperity

and the success that money can buy, those whose
riches shut them out from any vision of God
in a prison house of sensual selfishness, can speak
lightly of the magnificent protest of gurus and
monks, mystics and devotees. We of the West
with our boasted practicality have too often never
reached any freedom from self; rather we have
made selfishness our god, and settled down into
a complacent idolatry. But because we can make
the things of time and space our whole concern
and so lose our souls, the remedy does not necessarily lie along the negative road which leaves the
world unredeemed and irredeemable.

Jesus came at a time in which the two ideals were
at war. Rome was always, but then more than
usually, materialistic. No great race has ever been
so severely practical, so ruthlessly efficient, so
grossly sensual. Her religion, her philosophy, her
art, her poetry, her letters were all borrowed and
bought: like every *nouveau riche* she purchased
a culture which she had no power to create. The
Divus Augustus was a suitable deity for such a
folk. Against her stood the ascetics of the East,
pouring scorn upon her luxury and pomp, con-
signing all her world to Ahriman, withdrawing
from it as from a lazarhouse to the loneliness and
austerity, the vigils and speculations of Buddhist
and Magian, Essene and Gnostic. Disciplined by
fasting, weaned from human loves and hates as
beyond the reach of material interests, the sage
would strip himself of every contact with earth

that so in his hour of ecstasy he might have experience of the One, the infinite, the ineffable. Mankind was confronted with the choice between two worlds; one must be taken and the other left. Jesus alone refused to accept the alternative, The belief that He is Himself God and Man is wholly in keeping with His own insistence that here and now in nature and history, in the Universe of space and time God is Himself incarnate, that the two worlds are not antagonistic but intimately related, that the outward and visible is the expression and instrument of the inward and spiritual, and that life is not absorption in material ends nor in contemplative repose but a communion with God expressed and achieved in a passion of redemptive service for mankind.

Plato had declared that beyond illumination and the enjoyment of reality lay the illuminate's offering of himself in service to his fellows. He who had ascended out of the cave must freely descend again and spend himself to enlighten its prisoners. The very nature of the ideal good drives him back to work for goodness. Jesus went further. To Him there was not first a stage of contemplation and then a life of service : rather contemplation and service were alike the twofold source and fulfilment of life in God. If the knowledge of God is eternal life, this knowledge is achieved in the doing of the works. Vision and thought and action, heart and mind and will are not segregated in His life or His teaching. Our task is not to be imprisoned by things, nor to escape from them, but to consecrate and use them as what they are, the sacraments of God. Jesus points us to a way of life in which mankind, at one with God and in the fellowship of a single organism, shall be perfect as God is perfect, disclosing illimitable resources of energy in the fulfilment of love's enterprise and discovering that, for those who love, all things work together for good.

Such teaching is surely in accord both with our faith and with our experience.

(1) If God is Love, if He is what Jesus is, then an eternal activity of creation is His nature. Creation, redemption, inspiration, these are not three but one, aspects of a single process, manifestations of the love that brings many sons unto salvation. And life in God must involve for us not a passive accepttance but an active co-operation. We too in our little way and in communion with Him must create and redeem and inspire, suffering and serving as long as there are prodigals in the Father's family.

(2) In experience our moments of ecstasy are only valuable as they proceed from and give rise to an abounding and harmonious vitality, a quickened sense of value, a strengthened sympathy and kinship with all that is. At their highest such moments are not passive in quality. God is not merely our nurse to comfort and protect us : He takes us and fills us with an intense and throbbing

power, with an exquisite sensitiveness, a passion of love that rends away all the rags of our self-esteem and constrains us to a free and inevitable dedication for service. To live in Him is to be alert to all the beauty and order and friendliness of His world, to thrill with compassion and joy as we share its griefs and delights, to spend ourselves to the uttermost in an agony of effort which we cannot and would not avoid or diminish. It is in such unselfconscious effort that our lives are most truly eternal.

To release in us the full potentiality of the spirit there is needed not only a great loyalty, but a great opportunity. God in Jesus is revealed to us by the new knowledge of our day with a power to attract and satisfy and transcend all our aspirations: as we have learned to know Him better in the light of our clearer understanding of the world, of ourselves and of the gospel, so we should learn to appreciate more worthily His gifts of life and love. But love requires its occasion: if it is to be given full expression, it must be put to the test of a great adventure of service. It was not enough for the first disciples that the grandeur of the Crucified set them free from self and all its attendant weaknesses. This power of their consecration was only disclosed when they were entrusted with the quixotic task of world-evangelisation. Commissioned to undertake so stupendous a venture, every ounce of vitality was called into play; for men can only expend their uttermost when a crisis of superhuman magnitude confronts them. Then indeed they discover qualities undreamed of.

If we have eyes to see it, our own age would supply an opportunity not less overwhelming. To baptise the new knowledge, to formulate a synthetic theology, to interpret God in a fashion worthy of the art and science and ethics of to-day—there is a work to which every student whatever his branch of research should be proud to contribute. Quite plainly unless we can relate the new discoveries to some adequate scheme of philosophy, unless we can regain our hold upon the eternal realities of life, we shall continue to multiply distractions, to think and act compartmentally, to be at the mercy of the charlatan or the specialist : those whose sole concern is with some new thing, fall into the scepticism and the futility of the Athenians of St. Paul's day.

And along with the new knowledge we have to baptise the new social order. Education, industry, politics, racial and international contacts, in all of these there is the same need for fixed principles, for clear guidance, for a " new spirit." Experts are constantly pointing to the need for religion to supply both a common ideal and a common loyalty. In every department of human effort we have to discover first an agreed basis for a world-wide civilisation, and then how to bring our own calling into harmony with that basis. In the home, in the school, in shop and factory, bank and exchange, in council-chamber and parliament there is everywhere a clamant need for men who can rise above conventions and catchwords, who can discover the real issues beneath the mass of detail, and who can take a wide enough view of the situation to see their own work in relation to the best interests not of a class or of a nation but of mankind. And along with individual consecration there is need of a fellowship of effort so strong that in it we can meet and overcome corporate evils corporately.

It is ultimately true that the religion of the individual or of the community determines its character and destiny, that what we do is the outcome of what we believe. If we would meet the responsibilities of this obviously critical time, we can only do so by enlarging and deepening our hold upon God. And conversely if we are to strengthen and enrich our religion, we can best do so by confronting such a situation as now awaits us. In every aspect of life, in art and thought, in business and politics new problems await our solution. So vast are the issues that men have not hesitated to claim that they are insoluble and to predict the ruin of our civilisation in a welter of bankruptcy and blood. When men's hearts fail them for fear and for looking on the things that are coming upon the earth, then the soul of man looks up and takes courage : the summons that never comes in times of ease and prosperity rings out its message of good news : and men see in the storm and thick darkness the Son of Man coming in His Kingdom. We stand in a day of judgment ;

with God we can face it undismayed. And doing so we shall recover once more the romance of living eternally; the fortitude that no disaster can shake; the peace that is won by struggle; the joy that suffers; the love that abides. " Be of good cheer," said Jesus, " I have overcome the world "; and through the ages when a crisis has put their discipleship to the test His followers have proved the truth of His words.

There is indeed no room for fear or despondency, even as there is none for indifference or for selfishness. Vast as is the task, its grandeur makes it an inspiration and a challenge. Now for the first time in history we could see the fulfilment of the command of Jesus : " Go and make disciples of all the nations." Now for the first time mankind has become conscious of its unity and could realise its solidarity. We have a gospel adequate to man's need, resources sufficient for its fulfilment. Without God everyone of us is wretched, his life thwarted and incomplete : for fellowship every one of us, whatever our calling or capability, is needed : for service the opportunity is universal ; every one of us has something which only he can give. To worship God, to love one another, to serve and suffer together, those three are one, notes in the eternal chord which is man's part in the music of the spheres.

And in serving the immediate need of our own day we are helping to bring to its consummation a process infinitely more august. We are assisting in the age-long labour not of humanity only but of the whole cosmic process. As we look back upon evolution, we can trace in it the activity of the same eternal Spirit of whom Jesus is for us the unique manifestation, of whose method His Cross is the supreme symbol. The whole creation groaneth and travaileth until now, waiting for the coming of the sons of God, making ready for the emergence of the body of Christ. The opportunity won for us by the sacrifice of myriads of lowlier lives is ours, and "the Kingdom of God is at hand": we can take it if we "repent and believe the good news."

APPENDIX

A NOTE ON SCIENCE AND RELIGION

It may be objected by those who, like myself, make their approach to reality along the scientific lines of observation and induction, that the starting-point of this book should have been not man's highest experiences but his physiology. None of us nowadays is likely to underestimate the need for exact study of the evolution, character and processes of human life or the value of the contribution of biology and psychology. Every new discovery, whether it be of the function of endocrine glands or the nature of complexes, has its bearing upon the interpretation of religion; and a full theology should perhaps begin with a consideration of the bodily mechanism and the psychic make-up of mankind. My excuse for omitting this preliminary task must be that I have already surveyed it in my Hulsean and Noble lectures, *The Creator Spirit;* and that the agreement of many authorities as to the importance of "mystic" experience justifies me in taking it as a starting-point. Ultimately I believe that the fields of science and of religion will be found to coincide, that science cannot confine itself to the quantitative and that

religion must say *Humani nihil a me alienum puto.*
But meanwhile it is convenient on occasion to keep
the two modes of study distinct, provided that the
exponent of the latter sees to it that his theology
is not unscientific.

There may be some students of science, however,
who not only accept the definition which restricts
it to what can be observed by the senses, weighed
and measured, but who go on to the reckless
dogmatism which denies that anything not so
treated has any claim to consideration. Materialism
has since the time of Democritus always been
attractive to those who were exasperated by the
credulity and foolishness of much that passes for
religion, and who fear that if they once leave the
region where results can be " proved " in a labora-
tory they will have no basis nor criterion of judgment. And in an age of triumphant machinery
like our own it is natural that " when the human
mind invents or encounters the mechanistic theory
of the organism, it is confronted with an apparition
which it at once recognises as the darling of its
adolescence and the symbol of its power, a
machine." [1] Of late years materialistic theories
have appeared in several forms ; and most of us
have at one time or another, generally when we
were just beginning to think, been attracted by them.

Twenty years ago such materialism relied upon
heredity as its strong suit. Weismann's doctrine
of the isolation of the germ-plasm was held to

---

[1] Darbishire, *Introduction to a Biology*, p. 85.

prove that all development was literally the evolution or unrolling of potentialities locked up in the original germ-stuff. Mendel's law supplied an account of inheritance in terms of an unalterable determinism. De Vries' theory of mutations gave a convenient solution to the question how, if heritage is fixed, can change occur. It was assumed that mental no less than physical characters were fixed by heredity. And man became merely the product of his gametes—his ideals and virtues no less than the colour of his eyes being explicable in terms of the physics and chemistry of the germ-plasm.

Now Weismannism is no longer unchallenged; and indeed the whole position has been so severely shaken by further investigation that it can no longer be put forward as final or complete. So overwhelming has been the answer of philosophy to materialism that in England at any rate the struggle seemed over.

In the last few years, however, the American school of radical behaviourists has revived a materialistic doctrine on the lines laid down by Dr. J. B. Watson, their strong suit being Pavlov's investigations into the conditioned response. English psychologists have shown no signs of taking this school very seriously—have indeed dismissed it somewhat curtly as a mass of inconsistencies neither scientific in itself nor capable of explaining the real subject-matter of psychology. But as American propaganda has a way of drifting over to this country and being given more credit than it deserves, it will be well to survey it briefly. Dr. Dorsey's recent volume, *The Nature of Man*, may serve as an example.

The book is indeed well-calculated to appeal to the half-educated or to those in revolt against " superstition." It is brightly written, makes a great display of popular science, and conceals the weakness of its argument either by a fine refusal to press beyond the evidence or by adroit criticism of the follies of religion. In fact it is based upon a fallacy in argument. At the start Dr. Dorsey admits that " man is indeed more than a mere mechanism : " but in spite of this he sets out a mechanistic theory of man's nature, insists that this is all that science can consider, and then goes on to declare that mind, intelligence, soul, spirit, God are " figures of speech for the various forms of verbalised behaviour," " useless relics of an ignorant past," and that " fine arts, ethics, literature, moral values, intellectual pursuits are all on a par with fashions in hats," because on his mechanistic doctrine they can only be so regarded. But if man is not indeed only a machine, then his doctrine is incomplete, and he has no right to use it as final or to reject what is not reconcilable with it.

Though such a blunder is enough of itself to discredit this particular book, its position as a statement of the newest materialism may be worth fuller examination. Here heredity is totally abandoned : " Little is known of the laws of physical inheritance and nothing of so-called mental inheritance " : " Any normal new-born can learn anything " : physical and social environment determine genius and all individual differences.[1] Shades of Mendel, Galton, Bateson, what a claim in the name of modern science !

The emergence of life and the origin of its characteristic qualities are of course unexplained. " Because the molecules are big and complex they behave like dynamic mechanisms " and " Ages ago the injunction was laid upon animal protoplasm to explore its universe "—so are the greatest problems for the thinker airily dismissed ! Suffice it that it is " a mechanism of such complexity that it could rejuvenate itself, regenerate itself, build into itself simple compounds," and that from it in course of ages man has been evolved, since " when one-celled organisms became many-celled organisms certain cells took on special forms adapted to perform special work "—though how this change is to be explained is none too clear. Man has by evolution become " an extraordinarily sensitive mechanism, which could learn, which could retain what it had learned, which could profit by experience." He has a visceral mechanism with a preformed organisation so that it can begin to function after birth under the appropriate stimulus. He has no instincts, but as part of his innate and

[1] See pp. VIII, 75, 76, etc. P. 28 contradicts this. The book contains at least half a dozen similar self-contradictory statements.

APPENDIX

visceral equipment he has hate and fear reactions
whose mechanism is the adrenal gland, and a love
reaction in response to stimulus of the erogenous
zones. These reactions are inborn and not learned,
though they may be conditioned through experience. Along with this he has a motor mechanism
unorganised at birth but capable of learning, and
thus giving rise to kinæsthetic, manual or verbalised
behaviour. He learns by stimulus and response,
always and only through reflex arcs, and the variety
of response is due to experience. His thinking
is just talking to himself, " it is action in the voice
mechanism—mouth, throat, etc. ; but it is silent—
no sound is uttered ; and it is slight action only
—no movement in throat or mouth is perceptible."
We may note that this last admission means that
the whole hypothesis is on Dr. Dorsey's definition
unscientific, since science " holds that the knowable
is always within the range of man's observation,"
that is of his sense-organs : but as man certainly
thinks and yet according to the behaviourist has
no mind, the explanation may well be applauded
as at least ingenious.

Indeed for one who, like myself, is prepared to
accept the doctrine of " unrestricted concomitance,"
to allow that mechanistic analogies supply a valuable
picture of one aspect of reality, and to reject
vitalistic or animistic theories, it is not the attempt
to describe physiology in terms of stimulus and
response that I should criticise. Nor does it
greatly matter that many of Dr. Dorsey's dogmas

seem to me, scientifically speaking, unsound. My concern is solely to point out that materialism does not take us very far, that it fails to explain everything that is important in life, and that to declare it to be the sole hypothesis and on this ground to insist that " the school curriculum be relieved of most of its ' literature ' and of all its philosophy, ethics, morals, mind and religion," is an absurdity. In the particular book that we have been considering not only are all the most serious problems for the thinker evaded and all the finest products of man's achievement dismissed with scorn, but even so the author falls into a perpetual succession of inconsistencies. Not only are there contradictory statements made about nature, freedom, will, and heredity, but the main conclusion of the book is itself on its author's own showing illegitimate. For it is absurd at one time to deny that man has free will or mind by representing all his actions as mechanical responses to environment, and then to denounce the poor automaton in terms that ascribe to him freedom and mentality and control of his environment by statements like " Man, with his words and Words, assumes that he can outdo nature in furnishing incentives to live." The fact is that Dr. Dorsey, like most materialists and many superficial thinkers, supposes that when he calls mind a " central nervous system," or names a being that lives and grows and thinks and reproduces itself a " mechanism," or defines religion as " sugar and adrenalin," he can then dispense not only with the older words but with the realities to which they belong. He supposes that when he has explained so far as he can how a thing works he has explained the thing. And if anyone more philosophically inclined points out that this is a fallacy, the reply is to abuse philosophy.

It is of course hardly necessary to point out that a scientist as such is not necessarily qualified to expound a philosophy or to interpret the whole of reality. In point of fact he is usually a specialist with all the limitations that specialisation involves. Materialism is a good working hypothesis for the bio-chemist; by it he has already shown us some light upon the physical aspect of mental processes. We are not in the least anxious to challenge the evidence that man is immediately descended from an ape-like mammal and ultimately from a long chain of ancestry, still roughly " recapitulated " in his own embryonic development : nor do we doubt that the emotion of fear is associated with the liberation of adrenalin into the blood, or even that thought may have its physical concomitants in imperceptible movements of the voice-mechanism. What we dispute is that the whole truth about mankind or about fear and thought has been told by these discoveries, and that the analogy of a machine is adequate to express the total content of human experience. Such an analogy, if pressed, makes nonsense of all that is most real in human life ; even those who accept it as true have to live as if it were not : for it represents the physical structure as the only thing in humanity, a conclusion which no single human being believes except as a matter of theory : it leaves unexplained, or explained away, all the ends which make life valuable and all the motives which ennoble it : it reduces history to the most futile of puppet-shows : it is incompatible with any real belief in evolution : and wholly fails to account for the existence of the mind by which it was itself conceived.

That science and the mechanistic hypothesis have a great contribution to make to human welfare, that they have done much to rid religion of superstition and to force the religious to use reason instead of credulity, is splendidly true. As Christians we rejoice whole-heartedly in all honest enquiry even if in the course of it the enquirers are led to results which seem one-sided and incomplete. But when a scientist of to-day, unlike the vast majority of his brethren, seeks to revive materialism and force it upon us as the only adequate philosophy, then he must be told quite firmly that the claim has been overwhelmingly rejected, that it is proved unsound, and that until he can find adequate arguments or produce a single qualified philosopher to support him, it would be more seemly to stick to his own field of study.

For us in this country behaviourism seems singularly old-fashioned. Twenty years ago science was not merely mechanistic but confident that the universe itself and all human experience in it could be explained in terms of machinery and by analysis of its constituent elements. Since then the whole thesis has broken down: "biological developments, the doctrine of evolution, the doctrine of energy, and the molecular theories have rapidly undermined the adequacy of the orthodox materialism." [1] Scientists have abandoned what philosophers were never prepared to accept; and the result is a demand for a new interpretation of reality in terms rather of organisms than of matter, of wholes rather than parts. And with this is coming a new sense of the primary importance of religion. "The fact of the religious vision, and its history of persistent expansion, is our one ground for optimism." [2] When we find the evidence of one of the greatest mathematicians and most original thinkers reinforced by the conclusions of a great biologist and psychologist like Professor Lloyd Morgan, a great physicist like Professor Eddington, a great sociologist like Professor Urwick, and a great statesman like General Smuts (to mention only a selection of names), we may claim that a new era has begun. There is much confusion; the day for a complete synthesis is not yet: but it is inconceivable that we shall revert to materialism for our philosophy of the universe.

And for the Christian what is needed is a thankful recognition of the wonderful gifts that science

[1] Whitehead, *Science in the Modern World*, p. 165.
[2] p. 275.

has brought and will bring; a whole-hearted effort to understand and use those gifts as they bear upon our knowledge of God; and a resolve that we will learn and labour so to conceive and interpret our faith that our expression of it may be worthy of the best thought of the age. Scientists seeking to explain Nature are coming towards a conception of the Universe that leaves room for and indeed demands a belief in God. Christian scholars from their long study of the New Testament are reaching agreement about the teaching and significance of Jesus. There are abundant signs that the two lines of enquiry are coming together, that the re-discovered Christ explains and is explained by the meaning of the Natural Order. If that hope is fulfilled, and a truly synthetic theology formulated, the future of mankind will be bright indeed.

INDEX

STUDENT CHRISTIAN MOVEMENT

GOD IN THE COMMONPLACE: A Book
of Prayers. By J. S. HOYLAND, Author of *Prayers
for Use in an Indian College, etc.*   2s. 6d. net.

A collection of intimate prayers, welcoming, tracing or seeking the presence of God in the everyday events of human life.

CHILD PSYCHOLOGY AND RELIGIOUS
EDUCATION. By DOROTHY F. WILSON, B.Litt.
With a Preface by Canon B. H. STREETER.

4s. net ; paper, 2s. 6d. net.

A study of the psychology of childhood, and especially of
childhood's religion up to the age of twelve, with its bearing
upon the principles and methods of religious education. A
book of practical value to teachers and parents.

HUMANITY & LABOUR IN CHINA:
An Industrial Visit and its Sequel (1923-26). By
ADELAIDE MARY ANDERSON, D.B.E., M.A. Illus-
trated from original photographs.

Demy 8vo.   10s. 6d. net.

"Dame Adelaide Anderson has collected, with a zest for humane purposes
but never uncritically, a mass of data, both statistical facts for the econo-
mist and reformer, and human facts which have come under her acute
observation, which are shocking in themselves and terrible in their
implication."—*Times*.

THE QUIET ADVENTURE: A Book for
Boys about Prayer. By E. A. WILLIS, B.Sc. 2s. net.

SADHU SUNDAR SINGH: Called of God.
By Mrs PARKER.   5s. net ; paper, 3s. 6d. net.

"This is an unusual volume of fascinating interest. As we read it we
realise that the day of miracles is not past—that there is still such a thing
as Christian romance."—*Glasgow Evening Citizen*.

32 RUSSELL SQUARE, LONDON, W C. 1.

STUDENT CHRISTIAN MOVEMENT

JOHN BUNYAN. By R. H. Coats, M.A.

4s. net; paper, 2s. 6d. net.

"It is delightfully written by a man who knows his subject well, and understands the religious experience of the man of whom he is writing."— *Methodist Recorder.*

RATIONALISM AND ORTHODOXY OF TO-DAY: An Essay in Christian Philosophy. By J. H. Beibitz, M.A., sometime Vice-Principal of the Theological College, Lichfield. 5s. net.

"The argument of the book is stated confidently yet carefully, and it deserves appreciation for its competent handling of themes which lie at the heart of the Christian faith. . . . In the course of his argument Mr Beibitz offers a well-reasoned and acute criticism of Professor Julian Huxley's *Essays of a Biologist.*"—*Times Literary Supplement.*

RELIGION AND DRAMATIC ART. By Spencer Elliott, M.A. With a chapter on "Modern Drama," by C. F. Cameron, Dramatic Critic of the *Sheffield Daily Telegraph.* 4s. 6d. net.

"These chapters are full of an amazing erudition, but it is all learning lightly worn, for it is all extraordinarily pleasant to read. And no sensible person who knows anything about life will disagree with the writer's final conclusions. The drama is one of the great human interests, and it is the only possible attitude of intelligent religious people to use it for the best ends."— *Expository Times.*

THE ETHICS OF THE GOSPEL AND THE ETHICS OF NATURE. By the late H. H. Scullard, M.A., D.D., Professor of Church History and Christian Ethics, Hackney and New College, London. 10s. 6d. net.

"This is a book which students of Christian ethics cannot afford to neglect."—*Review of the Churches.*

LAUSANNE 1927: An interpretation of the World Faith and Order Conference. By Canon E. S. Woods. With a Preface by the Archbishop of Canterbury. 4s. net; paper, 2s. 6d. net.

A popular survey of the historic Conference at which the leaders of nearly every branch of the Christian Church throughout the world met to promote the cause of Christian unity.

32 RUSSELL SQUARE, LONDON, W.C. 1.